ENGAGING

FAMILIES

We want to especially thank Lakendra, Adrian, Cathy, and their families for giving us permission to share the details and delights of the two years we worked and learned together. Their support and partnership will reside as timeless reminders of the potential for home-school connections.

Lakendra and her mother, Janice.

Adrian and his mom, Debbie, and dad, Jerry.

Cathy and her family: Susan (mom), Terry (dad), and Charlie (brother).

ENGAGING

FAMILIES

Connecting Home

and School

Literacy

Communities

Betty Shockley
Barbara Michalove
JoBeth Allen

Foreword by Donald H. Graves

Heinemann
Portsmouth, NH

TO OUR PARENTS
Luby and Floy Bell of Goldsboro, North Carolina (*Betty Schockley*)
Adele and Leonard Michalove in Atlanta, Georgia (*Barbara Michalove*)
Pete and Gene Paine in BellaVista, Arkansas, formerly of Hill City, Kansas
(*JoBeth Allen*)

**ALSO TO THE FAMILIES OF FOWLER DRIVE ELEMENTARY
SCHOOL, ATHENS, GEORGIA**

AND WITH BEST WISHES TO YOU AND YOURS

Heinemann
A division of Reed Elsevier Inc.
361 Hanover Street   Portsmouth, NH 03801-3912
Offices and agents throughout the world

The authors and the publisher would like to thank the teachers, children, and
parents who have given their permission to include material in this book. Every
effort has been made to contact the copyright holders and the children and their
parents for permission to reprint borrowed material. We regret any oversights
that may have occurred and would be happy to rectify them in future printings of
this work.

Library of Congress Cataloging-in-Publication Data
Shockley, Betty.
   Engaging families : connecting home and school literacy communities / Betty
Shockley, Barbara Michalove, JoBeth Allen ; foreword by Donald H.
Graves.
      p.   cm.
   Includes bibliographical references.
   ISBN 0-435-08845-9 (acid-free paper)
   1. Home and school—United States.   2. Education, Elementary—
Parent participation—United States.   3. Language arts
(Elementary)—United States.   4. Family literacy programs—United
States.   I. Michalove, Barbara.   II. Allen, JoBeth.   III. Title.
LC225.3.S55   1995
372.6—dc20   94-49151
                                                                    CIP

Editor: Carolyn Coman
Cover design: Jenny Greenleaf, Julie Hahn
Front-cover art: "Families" by Brenda Joysmith
Copyright © Joysmith Studios, Emeryville, CA
Printed in the United States of America on acid-free paper.
99 98 97 96 95 EB 5 4 3 2 1

CONTENTS

Issues of Policy and Practice

FOREWORD

Good teachers have always seen the importance of the parent role in their child's learning. There's nothing new about advocating strong connections between home and school. What is new is that a team of professionals from Georgia—Betty Shockley, Barbara Michalove, and JoBeth Allen—have shown how to redefine teacher-parent relationships to the mutual aid of both, and have written a book about it. This book, *Engaging Families: Connecting Home and School Literacy Communities,* details two years' worth of literacy-related transactions between teachers and parents. This is not a book *about* school-home communication. Rather, we have samples of the actual communications themselves: teacher to parent, parent to teacher, teacher to child, child to parent. We see changes in the literacy of teachers, parents, and children growing out of the mutual respect each has for the other.

The authors state at the beginning: "We set out to establish a partnership, not a program." The partnership is based on parallel practices where teachers, children, and parents build trust to talk simply and directly about literacy and learning at home and at school. Letters and journals go back and forth between them. Above all the school wants to learn "the things parents do at home that make their children better learners" and "what we can do together" for the sake of the child. The tone and content of the letters reflect an attitude of one learner sharing with another learner.

"I have so little time to actually teach." This is one of the more familiar cries I hear in teachers' rooms across the country. Teachers are frustrated by the burden of annual additions of new curriculum, and of days punctuated by constant interruption. These teachers seem to say, "The less time we have, the more we need to enlist the aid of parents." I was struck by how the authors extended time in school to include the home—through parents reading to children, and through children reading to brothers, sister, grandparents, or neighbors. Indeed, they have redefined the meaning of "time on task" in the best sense.

The authors say, "Teachers are like single parents." They are quite alone in their quest to help children learn, with few professionals to discuss the daily learning of the children. Shockley, Michalove, and Allen are not alone. From day to day they communicate with the extended family of the classroom, celebrating breakthroughs in learning, the completion of a book, a child's ability to read, or the joy of grandparents listening to grandchildren read. I could feel the energy in these letters as each couldn't wait to celebrate some new learning. There's a lot of literate gossip here about learning, the best kind.

Participants in this book are busy people (teachers and parents) who have found the means to cooperate together for the sake of their children. These are not parents from an upper-middle-class, wealthy community with high levels of educational attainment. Rather, these are eager middle-class parents, many of whom are European Americans and African-Americans. Some maintain two or three jobs, are unemployed, or travel extensively through the military. Some parents are alone and are forced to return home from work late in the evening. Yet they all read to their children and write letters to or exchange journals with the teacher. In some cases the letters are halting and demonstrate a struggle with spelling and word choice. But the desire to communicate with teachers—who eagerly await news of the children's learning—far transcends any reluctance to write.

This book is one of the best I have seen to date that demonstrates the function of literacy. Reading and writing are tools to connect people; parents, teachers, and children construct knowledge together. A child listens with classmates to a story his or her parent has written. Letters spawn family stories and those stories are told in class; some are oral, some are written. At every turn, in home and at school, the child witnesses the demonstration of literacy's function.

Scholars have written from both sides of the data about the necessity of partnerships between parents and schools. Denny Taylor and Catherine Dorsey Gaines' work, *Growing Up Literate* (1988), certainly shows the potential for literate growth within the home. Shirley Brice Heath, in *Ways with Words* (1983), shows the power and potential of storytelling, especially in her Trackton families, and she has long advocated the possibilities of partnerships between home and school. In addition, many specially funded programs have worked to bring home and school together. Finally, in *Engaging Families,* the book you are about to read, we see the exciting possibilities of literacy between equals, parents and teachers, which enhances the dignity of each.

References

Heath, Shirley Brice. 1983. *Ways with words*. Cambridge: Cambridge University Press.

Taylor, Denny, and Catherine Dorsey-Gaines. 1988. *Growing up Literate*. Portsmouth, N.H.: Heinemann.

Donald H. Graves

AUTHORS' NOTE

This book is related to a National Reading Research Center project of the University of Georgia and the University of Maryland (PR/AWARD NO. 117A20007) as administered by the Office of Educational Research and Improvement, U.S. Department of Education.

While we are grateful for their support, our findings and opinions do not reflect the position or policies of the National Reading Research Center, the Office of Educational Research and Improvement, the U.S. Department of Education, or the International Reading Association.

FOCUS ON RELATIONSHIPS

ONE

Respecting and Learning from Families

You should have seen Brandon the morning Betty read his mother's story to the class. He positioned himself in the middle of his classmates as they huddled expectantly on the floor around her. Instead of sitting in the conventional manner—legs crossed, face forward—Brandon curled down over his knees, placing his hands on top of his head as if to keep his body from popping up uncontrollably like a jack-in-the-box whose spring was wound too tight. As Betty read aloud his mother's contribution to our class book of family stories, he could not contain his excitement. He giggled in expectation, leaped up laughing at times, and at the conclusion sighed, "I can't believe my mom wrote that!" In fact, the story became legendary within our class community because no one wanted to be "monkey for a week!"

You should have seen Betty each morning as she read each home-school reader response journal. She too had a difficult time containing her joy as she saw children and parents building relationships around books. Invariably the stack of tablets would reveal some new insights recorded by either the children or the parents. Many of them were as touching as the following entry from Brandon's journal in which his mother gained a glimpse of her efficacy as a parent. She wrote:

February Wednesday 12, 1992
Book: The Cow That Went Oink

How Brandon saw this story interested me greatly. Brandon said that it was a sad story because the other animals laughed at the cow and the pig because they were different. He said he was glad because it ended the way it did. I've taught Brandon *never* to laugh at anyone because they are different, and to never laugh at anyone's misfortune. I'm glad that he applied my teachings to this story. It shows that he "really" takes to heart the things I say.

Entries like this let Betty (first grade) and the next year Barbara (second grade) know they had found a way to reach out and invite families in. We could all begin to know each other as people who read and write. As Adrian's mom told us, "You didn't have to wait for conference time to find out what was really going on. You had a way to communicate every day." By including families in our community, we made our classrooms closer and richer places. We were able to experience daily the reciprocal nature of the three Rs of language arts: reading, writing, and relationships.

Donna Skolnick, in her article "Reading Relationships" (1992), discussed Seymour Sarason's four primary relationships that affect the quality of life in a classroom:

- Relationships between the teacher and the student
- Relationships between the teacher and the curriculum
- Relationships between the student and the curriculum
- Relationships between and among the students

We think there is a need to consider additional levels of involvement that significantly affect classroom communities and individual members of those communities:

- Relationships between the parents and the curriculum
- Relationships between the teacher and the parents
- Relationships between the parents and the children
- Relationships between readers and books

In addition, we suspect that what Nancie Atwell said about the power of imposed programs such as basals to "distance teachers from students and distort the processes we hope they will learn" has an equally distancing effect on parents. This kind of instruction often perpetuates a mismatch between school and home literacy events and expectations. In *Side by Side* (1991, p. xvi), Atwell urged teachers "to become more active both in the classroom and out of it, to move beyond method, and to sit side by side with students as observers of learning and participants in writing and reading." Having made this move professionally out from behind teachers' manuals to face students as individual learners, we wanted to offer parents the opportunity to witness and participate in their own children's literacy journey in much the same way. After all, who can better sit side by side with their youngsters?

Caring families

However, current conventional wisdom tells us that "many parents just don't care anymore." Teachers decry this condition by announcing, "If parents did a better job parenting, we teachers wouldn't have such a difficult time teaching." Our experience directly contradicts this "wisdom." All the families of these classes, families with a wide range of literacy abilities, wrote to tell us about their children and participated in our *Family Stories* (1992) project in addition to supporting our regular homework practice of reading and writing in journals together.

So, who were these families? If all these families were so involved, was this a private school? A highly educated, middle-class suburban community where parents had time and resources to spare? One evening at a parent meeting we asked the five African American and four European American parents in attendance to provide us with a description of the school. We write about it frequently and are often asked to describe this population. We were tired of and somewhat uncomfortable with the usual percentage descriptors of black and white families, free lunch, parental schooling, and so on.

Parents wrote for a few minutes and then shared their descriptions. These didn't have anything to do with percentages. They spoke of the school as "an extended family," "progressive," "a neighborhood learning center" where "parents are welcome" and there is "rapport between teachers and administration." They described the families who attend as "parents who are really, really trying to do our best—even if it means doing laundry at 9:00 [p.m.] and the kid's sitting on the dryer reading to me," "many single-parent families," "poor to middle class," with "everybody pulled in a lot of different directions." The most common descriptor of both school and families was "caring." One parent even commented, "I don't see this school by race or anything but as a whole community working to make this school the best." Were these exceptional families? Yes. But aren't all families?

This discussion supported the advice Denny Taylor and Catherine Dorsey-Gaines gave readers in *Growing up Literate* (1988):

> If we can change our perceptions of families with children living in poverty so that we behave a little differently at the axis of behavior where we locate policy and justice, if we can convince ourselves that the myths and stereotypes that create images of specific groups (inner-city families, teenage mothers and their children) have no relevance when we stop counting and start observing and working with people, then we will have nudged the world a little. And if we can persuade others that sex, race, economic status, and setting cannot be used as significant correlates of literacy, the writing will have been worthwhile. (p. xx)

From the beginning, our work together assumed wonderful things about children, families, and literacy. We believed that all children want to learn, that all families want to support that learning, and that the road to literacy can and should be an enjoyable one. We were not disappointed.

In setting our scene, we invite you to visit our town, Athens, Georgia, and our school, Fowler Drive Elementary. Betty and Barbara taught first and second grades, respectively, at Fowler Drive, and JoBeth is a professor in the Language Education Department at nearby University of Georgia. We bring unique perspectives to the writing and development of this book. Betty taught the first group of first graders and began again with a new group of first graders, while Barbara got to know the students and families from the first year as they all became second graders in her class. JoBeth offered an outsider's perspective that helped us balance our subjective and objective viewpoints.

You as readers will bring your own viewpoints to this book. Some of you are teachers, some are parents, some are both—as we three are. Now that the parents have introduced you to the feel of the school and its families, we'd like you to visualize a familiar scene.

Many mornings it's barely light as the train of boxy, yellow school buses pulls around the Fowler Drive traffic circle. Brakes whine and engines cough exhaust before a final wheezing breath of the door releases waking travelers into a new day of school. Teachers stand in greeting and wonder what life has been like since yesterday for the children who file past in dimlit review.

Teachers are not the only ones who wonder about children: family and friends at the other end of the line have questions too. "What did you do at school today?" they ask. More often than not, their invitations are answered with a shrug and "nothing." Artifacts of schooling are excavated from the daily debris of cartoon-character book bags in an often futile attempt to piece together the unspoken memories.

Meaningful connections

How do we strengthen the connections between the days and the nights, the chugs and stalls of learning, the choppy stops and starts of home and school routines? How do we make more free-flowing the routes of reasoning and the paths of practice? Finding ways to create such bridges has been a concern on school reform agendas locally and nationally for quite some time. We read about it in the newspaper. We hear it again and again at Parent Teacher Organization meetings. We know it's important, but we struggle with how to make it happen. Recently a group of teachers, school administrators, and university professors were gathered for a School Research Consortium meeting.* One group was discussing home-school connections and the issues of creating shared understanding. A portion of that conversation might serve to clarify some of the reasons that responding to a recognized need is not as easy as it might seem:

Emily Carr (kindergarten teacher): What do we mean by the home-school connection? Is it, "Let me show you how to be like me?"

Maxine Easom (elementary school principal): I worry about how do we offer parent involvement . . . involving parents in their children's learning . . . not in serving the school . . . what we've interpreted from our white, middle-class background as volunteer time.

Beth Tatum (high school English teacher): How can I open the door of communication? Can I do that without talking to every single parent on the phone?

Maxine (principal): I worry I don't have enough energy to do all I want to do.

Beth (high school): I know now I didn't really trust my seniors to talk about their books with their families. That's why I gave them that list of suggestions. Betty [whose son, Jamie, had been in her class that year] told me later that [my questions] really got in the way of their conversation because Jamie took my suggestions as law. He kept checking the list to see if they had covered everything so he could get a good grade.

Emily (kindergarten): Giving them a chance to talk about books is so important. People tend to perceive books and reading as such a solitary thing.

Gay Williford (Chapter 1 teacher): I want to try with my Chapter 1 classes what Betty did with her home journals.

Maxine (principal): Why do you want to do it?

Gay (Chapter 1): Because in a lot of cases there's no *obvious* interest or concern on behalf of the child. If we start with this response, maybe they'll learn to look forward to it. It's like opening the door to interacting with the school. I'm concerned, though, that I'll do it right.

Emily (kindergarten): If you hear your teacher voice coming through—beware; look for an honest response. They're going to influence what happens at school. Try to honestly communicate and learn.

Gay (Chapter 1): I wonder what are the things that parents do at home that make their children better learners? What can we do together? What can we try?

---

*All three of us are researchers within the SRC, which is a major strand of the National Reading Research Center. Betty Shockley is the SRC coordinator and principal investigator of this group of forty researchers, mostly teachers.

Echoes of this conversation can be heard throughout the country in homes, in schools, in school board offices, wherever people gather who care about education. Here we gain a glimpse of how issues of time ("I worry I don't have enough energy to do all I want to do") and accessibility ("Can I do that without talking to every single parent on the phone?") can impede action. A core concern is which model of literacy could be used to guide such work, as Emily worried about the usual stance of educators ("Let me show you how to be like me"). Anxieties about "doing it right," learning to be "open-minded," and "looking for an honest response" are ongoing professional struggles. Two things seem sure: we need to find ways to access more directly "the things parents do at home that make their children better learners," and we need to communicate "what we can do together."

Betty, Barbara, and JoBeth hope that by sharing in this book some of the details, dilemmas, and delights of the home-school connections we created, in partnership with children and their families, we might provide examples of how to begin. This is an invitation to consider and to act rather than wait for local or state mandates. You, as teachers and parents, can adopt elements of our practices as starting points for your own efforts to build stronger relationships between home and school. The key to success is respect and an openness to learn with and from all concerned. We must set aside preconceived notions of "the one right way" and listen to one another so that we might construct together a more flexible and personally sensitive way of responding to changing needs and issues.

Kindergarten teacher Karen Hankins, a teacher-researcher colleague, captured this insight when she wrote about her ongoing attempts to connect with families affected by drug and alcohol dependence:

> Home visits are rich and invaluable experiences. I have done home visits for years as a matter of course. But going in as a researcher gave me new eyes. In my journal, after reading *Ways with Words* [Heath, 1983], I wrote, "Today I look at Rodney, Loretta, and Nat with new eyes. Eyes asking questions, ears ready to hear. Yesterday, I wanted to give out answers—how pious—today, it's different. Asking myself what I can learn about reading and writing from Rodney gave me new vision, and at the same time, fear. What if I fail? Not, what if Rodney fails, but, what if I miss the connection? What if I forget that baby steps will eventually lead one home, just as giant steps do?" As I made my home visits, I knew that I had gone not to teach but to learn.

Our story goes beyond parent involvement or parent participation to a partnership. The characters are teachers, students, and families who care about literacy and each other. As writers of our own literate histories, we recognized the importance of the transfer of traditions through story. By making pathways explicit between the stories of home and the stories of school, we enriched and included both communities. We replaced the traditional process of denial and exclusion perpetuated by quiet, no-talking, fill-in-the-blank routines at school with dynamic interchanges such as daily storytelling times, home-school reader response journals, family story writing, and opportunities for reflection.

As a result of our partnership, nobody was alone anymore. The teachers no longer felt the sole responsibility for educating the children. The families had concrete ways to participate that were meaningful and generated trust. The children knew their school and homes were united in purpose and position, and they developed trust in the compatibility of learnings. These were hope-giving experiences. Mem Fox, one of our _ favorite picture book authors, reminded us, "When it comes to literacy, the relationship is the most important thing" (1992, p.74). In the process of becoming literate, it matters when children have relationships with books they love and people they love.

Our book describes two groups of children and their families: Betty's first graders, who became Barbara's second graders, and a new group of first graders (see Appendix B). The partnerships formed that first year in first grade were continued in second grade, and another partnership continued as well: the teaching relationship between Betty and Barbara. Because Betty and Barbara shared a whole language philosophy of education and a core respect for children and families as learners and co-teachers, there was strong continuity between the first and second grades for all concerned. Every day in school the children chose books they wanted to read and focused their writing on topics of their own choosing. They had extended periods of time in which to pursue areas of interest, and they worked with Betty and Barbara in designing a curriculum that met their needs. However, because Betty had felt for years that she had been excluded from the real "goings on" of her own children's education, she was committed to including the parents of her students in their children's education. She designed a set of parallel practices (see Chapter 3) that attempted to honor the voices (Oldfather, 1993) of children, teachers, and families as they also built connections between the whole language practices of the classroom and the literacy practices of home.

Respectful dialogue

First grade is an especially "big deal" for children and the people who love them. It's the year children expect to learn to read and write and start having real homework. On the first day of school Betty sent home an invitation to parents to "tell me about your child." She received in return heartfelt scenarios about the lives and loves of each of her students. Soon after, the children and their families began a thrice-weekly dialogue process with one another through their reader response journals. The journals were a nonthreatening place to communicate. Our comments as teachers were supportive and demonstrated a belief in the efficacy of parents as their children's first teachers. There was obvious respect for individual differences, for children, and for family decisions about literacy and how to use the journal.

Perhaps best of all, the journal gave children a chance to see this mutual respect developing, families respecting teachers, teachers respecting families, and both respecting the child as a unique learner. Betty admired and respected Anthony's family as they found ways to stay connected to school despite difficult times. "I wondered if I would have been so responsible and supportive if I had been in their shoes," she marveled. Anthony's home burned to the ground that year, and the family lost everything. His grandmother died. His mother was not able to find employment. Yet twenty-three times during the year, a family member wrote in the journal, usually his mom. By second grade, his twelve-year-old sister, Amanda, had taken over many responsibilities involving Anthony, including writing in his journal with him. Although both attendance and homework were sporadic, Anthony's sisters and cousins continued to be involved with the journal until Anthony was responding independently, in April of second grade.

The children were also respected as readers. This seemed critical to many children. One was Bryan, who loved animals, especially dinosaurs. Through informational book choices, he was able to learn more about them, and he often included bits of information in his responses, as befits an informational book. Colin loved funny books and was quick to reject books that were not funny, as he did when he wrote, "This does not fit into my category of books." He progressed from joke books and *Mad* magazine to John Scieszka's *Time Warp Trio* and Roald Dahl's *The BFG* and other writings.

Additionally, the parents wrote stories about their family experiences and published them in a class book of *Family Stories* (1992) to be shared and read over and over again both at school and at home. Parents and students participated equally at the end of the year in a set of daily reflections about learning to read and write, and sharing in the process. Their responses in conjunction with our extensive and varied records of literacy development led to informed instructional decision making.

Parents' assessments

Parents and children knew this had been important work. Renee's mother, in response to an end-of-year request to tell us how she thought her child learned to read, wrote the following confirming view: "60% of her learning was from her teacher, and 40% was from at home with her parents." When Betty asked Adam how he'd learned to read so well, he said immediately, "My mom taught me. You know when you send those books home at night—my mom reads them to me, and sometimes I read to her." Another interesting facet of the journals and family stories occurred to us when LaToya wrote in her journal: "My mom is a good writer Ms. Shockley is too." Children don't routinely see their parents as writers. Brad's mom wrote, "Brad loves for me to read to him not only his homework [books from school] but whatever novel, magazine or newspaper I may be reading. He sits quietly and listens to the stories I read because I change my voice for different parts and try to act out the stories that are long."

In the end, it was Dennis' mom who touched our hearts and opened our eyes to the tremendous potential of sharing the love and responsibility of learning. One morning when the children had gone for their half-hour art class and Betty was settling into her routine of having coffee and responding in the journals, there it was—the essence of our partnership:

> Dennis read really good I only told him about 4 or 5 words. when he finished reading I clapped my hands and gave him a big kiss on the cheek, and told him he did great. he's really becoming a smart child. I was just thinking to myself. If a child has a wonderful teacher and wonderful parents that takes up time with him and helps him to read and learn new things he turns out to be a genius. what I think my little Dennis will be someday.

So we ask you, is it possible for this first grader to leave behind his early labels of Chapter 1 and S.I.A. (Special Instructional Assistance), in a system that does not always serve African American males well, to emerge as a genius just because his teachers and parents are "wonderful"? We would ask you to believe it could be so. Believing that Dennises can become geniuses will be necessary, if only for the purpose of understanding this book, although we hope the view will become more long-lasting.

We ask you to risk this belief, which flies in the face of so much "conventional wisdom," those who say knowingly that "he really doesn't have a chance," and "the schools can't really make a difference when the kids come in so behind," and, of course, "parents just don't care anymore." Even some people who have read the journals have continued their deficit views. An administrator was surprised that some of the "more educated parents" had not written more extensively or often, or gotten their children to write more "correctly"; we marveled at parents' focus on meaningful content and ability in some cases to overcome their own writing inhibitions. A professor wondered at the low rate of "task completion" and involvement by some parents; we applauded children who became increasingly responsible for writing in the journals, and learned that many family members found other ways to share their children's literacy. We welcome your risk taking by continuing with us. We hope this book helps you complete that route with the yellow school buses, so that it will no longer be a one-way trip carrying your children home or delivering them at the school door. Rather, with us, you will begin to see the complete circle, home to school to home.

TWO

Partners in Literacy: Home and School

Teacher-researcher Emily Carr wrote that being a teacher is like being a single parent (Carr and Allen, 1989). You have no one to talk with about a child's everyday triumphs and traumas or decisions about how to help the child, no one to share your smile when the child says something delightful, insightful, or just plain silly. Being a parent is often as isolated as teaching. Whether in a one- or two-parent family, you are often the only one there for moment-by-moment decisions, crises, and joys. Neither parent nor teacher gets much feedback either. It's rare that anyone takes the time to say, "You're doing a great job of raising this child," or "Your teaching is really making a difference in my child's life." Yet these are exactly the kinds of messages we shared, not with one family but with many, not once a year but regularly through two years.

We are teachers and parents who have felt the loneliness and weight of making decisions by ourselves on behalf of our own children and other people's children. For *Engaging Families,* we thought from our parental perspective about how we would like to have a voice in our children's school lives; then we acted from our teaching perspective to find ways of connecting home and school. We are not suggesting that the ways we found are the ways that will be best for others. Rather, we hope this book will help you find your own ways of building partnerships.

From *Engaging Children* to *Engaging Families*

In *Engaging Children* (Allen, Michalove, and Shockley 1993), a three-year case study of six children whom Betty and Barbara worried about the most, we became interested in developing meaningful home-school connections. All the children we studied made unsolicited reference to home literacy events, including being read to or encouraged to read; literacy was valued in each home. But we had no way to gain specific insights into what families valued and practiced, and no way for families to gain insights into how their children were becoming literate in school.

In that study, we identified "stability" as an important theme, a finding that became evident as both the school and home worlds became insecure and unstable for the children through retention, mandated school transfers, a succession of substitute teachers, and family crises. Bronfenbrenner (1979) postulated that it is when children move from one primary setting to another that they have the greatest potential for either

11

growth or alienation. Such opportunities (or risks) include moving from home to school, grade to grade, or school to school. Whether children grow or become alienated depends on two factors, according to Bronfenbrenner. The first is the fit between primary settings: how much adjustment will be necessary. The second is the extent to which the new settings are "open or closed to the developing person" (p. 288). We felt strongly, from our study, that we (the school) were not doing enough to create that fit between home and school, and that we could be more open and supportive of the developing children in our care if we knew more about them and had specific connections with their families.

Betty designed the parallel practices detailed in Chapter 3. Throughout that first year, when *Engaging Families* was not yet a study but first and foremost good practice, Betty shared her excitement with Barbara and JoBeth. She read excerpts from journals and letters from parents telling her about their child, and explained her detailed literacy records that clearly showed real progress by each child. As we contemplated the difficulties of extending the *Engaging Children* case studies to a fourth year, discussing how our questions might change as the children moved into middle school, Barbara said, "You know what my question really is? My question is, how would the things you've done in first grade to connect with families work in second grade?" A new study was born.

We collected and analyzed data (see Appendix B) from Betty's first grades for two years, and from Barbara's second grade (the same group of children from Betty's first year). At our research team meetings, we regularly asked each other, "What are these data a study of? What's this story mainly about?" We decided that it was a study of communication among families, children, and teachers, about expectations, concerns, and the child as a learner. The partnerships that formed supported and extended authentic literacy learning; we learned what was "real" at home, families learned what was "real" at school, and children extended their literacy networks and their choices in both settings.

One reason we feel our research partnership was effective was that we had both the "insider's view" that teachers bring to school-based research and an "outsider's view" (Erickson, 1986). Betty was the teacher who had generated the first year's data; she had a year-long relationship with the children and families through which to interpret journals, reflections, and so on. Barbara was the teacher who currently taught the children and interacted with the families; she was able to update the previous year's data with current information about how the child was developing, what pattern the second grade journal was taking, and so forth. JoBeth was the outsider who did not know the children or their families; she asked questions that led us beyond the "taken for granted," and she helped make the familiar strange for Betty and Barbara. They did the opposite for her. Together, we generated and modified assumptions about ourselves, the children, and their families. The following are those that held true across the data.

Assumptions about ourselves as teachers

When we learned from families, we made more informed decisions on behalf of children.

When we recognized parents as their children's first teachers, we learned to count on families as co-teachers; there was shared accountability and security in knowing each child had one-to-one time with "a more capable peer" (Vygotsky, 1978) who was a supportive family member.

When we listened to and read family stories and journal entries, we developed "funds of knowledge for teaching" (Moll et al., 1992).

When we saw children through their families' eyes in addition to our own, we saw them in ways that helped us teach the whole child more completely.

When families corresponded in the journals, they kept their children at the forefront of our thinking. No one got lost, no one was able to hide—each had constant visibility.

Because we respected the families, we learned to follow their lead for how they chose to use the journals.

We used the journals to share information about literacy development in general, and specific suggestions for individual children, based on our own kid watching (both at our homes and at school).

We came to see what we are about as learner-centered educators—not teacher-centered, or even student-centered, but centered on all of us as learners.

Assumptions about families

All these families cared about their children, just as we care about ours.

They wanted to be involved. If they had not been involved with the school in the past, perhaps it was because the opportunities had been token or one-way (school informing or "training" parents; see Chapter 11). In contrast, these were genuine invitations, no strings or certificates attached, no grades, no evaluation, constant feedback and acceptance.

Parallel practices seemed to offer families a meaningful role no matter how comfortable they were with their own literacy. All families participated in some way—those who read widely, those who did not or could not read, and those who saw reading with their children in terms of their own previous school-like teacher question/child answer sessions, as did some parents in Heath's (1983) study of home and school literacy.

The journal process supported and developed many parents' sense of efficacy, both as parents and as teachers.

Families seemed to develop an increased respect for their children as readers and writers, both from the regular interaction with them around texts and from the teacher's words of respect for their children and celebration of their unique abilities and areas of growth.

Parents seemed to appreciate the teacher's support for many difficult decisions they had to make, both as parents and as their children's home teachers; many entered into a teaching/learning partnership with both the child and the teacher.

Family members often provided very explicit literacy instruction. Many had a repertoire of literacy support strategies; they would nudge, back off, press, and encourage children to feel successful. Most scaffolded their support in close harmony with children's signaled needs. Occasionally the interactions became stressful, but the journal often served as a way of changing to more enjoyable interactions.

Assumptions about children

Children dramatically extended their literacy engagement because of time spent reading and writing one-to-one with family members.

Children extended their literacy networks; they read and wrote with a wide variety of people at home and at school. They got to know each other as readers and writers, and each other's *families* as readers and especially as writers through family stories.

Children grew as readers and writers.

Children grew in their ways of responding to literature and in their literary conversations, both oral and written.

Children saw the adults closest to them—their families and teachers—actively engaged in reading and writing.

These assumptions continue to evolve and to advance our inquiry. Revising and revisiting our assumptions kept visible issues that might otherwise have faded out of analysis, just as reading the journals kept each child visible to us as teachers.

Stability, engagement, and community

In *Engaging Children* we identified the importance of stability, engagement, and community. After studying the partnerships in *Engaging Families,* we developed a broader perspective of the scope of each, and multiple perspectives on each element of literacy.

Stability at and between home and school

We saw from family perspectives the importance of a stable, reliable homework format; the parents did not have spelling words one night, math problems the next, and a report on weasels hanging over their heads for a week. Every night they knew they would have a book their child had chosen; they would read, talk, and, two or three times a week, write. Peterson, in describing in *Life in a Crowded Place* (1992) how he and students created classroom communities, points to the importance of individual routines. Each family created its own routine with storybooks and the journals. Some read right after school, some before bedtime, some while the other parent fixed supper; some read on the couch, others bedside, and one child sat on the dryer and read to her mother as she did the laundry. As we will see in the Family Portraits section, the dynamics during reading and writing changed with time and the child's growing literacy abilities. But the important routine of taking time together to read and talk about books was a dependable part of each family's life.

In addition to adding to the stability of children's home lives, we were able to create stability in their school lives in two ways. First, we established community routines that included time to read, write, and share their responses to the writings of various authors including themselves, and time to bring family stories into the classroom collection of oral and written texts. Second, we created continuity between the children's first- and second-grade years by getting permission for the class to stay together as it moved from Betty's room to Barbara's room. This was important not only in terms of maintaining the established community understandings and rapport but also because as teachers we shared a strong, verbalized and actualized philosophy of children and learning. Our students walked into second grade able to write about topics they had selected as personally meaningful and converse about (talk *and* listen) books in terms of personal connections, intertextual connections, author's style, and genre. They also came expecting to take books home to read with their parents, and they were pleased with their new, but still familiar, response journals.

Finally, we added to children's overall stability through the partnership each family created with us. Families and teachers provided connected experiences: families _ told and wrote stories; children saw adults reading and writing in both settings; families, teachers, and children reflected on past learning and planned new ways to grow. These parallel practices were moving us much closer to that fit between the primary settings of home and school that Bronfenbrenner (1979) saw as critical for children to develop most fully.

An extended engagement

At a very simple but powerful level, parallel practices meant that children spent more time engaged in reading, writing, and literate talk. For a more complex framework for examining engagement, we turned to whole language educator and theorist Brian Cambourne (1988). From studying engaged learners, he described four essential elements of engagement: learners as potential doers, learning as personally meaningful, learning as low risk, and learners bonding with other doers.

Before they are willing to engage in a new venture, learners have to see themselves as potential doers. Being doers meant for both adults and children in our extended learning community being readers, writers, storytellers, and evaluators. We intentionally opened the door as wide as possible so that families could create formats they felt comfortable with—formats for reading, responding, and writing that allowed everyone to be a doer. We did not provide initial models or issue format constraints on journals or family stories; we wrote open-ended reflection questions for both family and child to think about. Thus, some families wrote lengthy family stories, whereas others provided nuggets of family wisdom; some families responded in the journals using pictures or copied text.

How do people come to see themselves as doers? Undoubtedly, families became involved because they had genuine and open-ended invitations with high expectations from Betty and Barbara that they were capable doers and important teachers for their children, and because journals and family stories were, after all, homework. Additionally, Peterson (1992) observed that in many of life's events, people become doers by "parading." He developed the insight when he took a class of children to watch a parade. "Not content to stand by and watch the parade, the children joined it from the inside to experience it as best they could" (p. 86). Peterson further explained:

> Paraders are involved in making, doing, performing. . . . People of all ages . . . join and give themselves to the experience, participating as the spirit and interest moves them. In parading there are no fixed models of behavior to be reproduced or standards to be met. (p. 86)

We think we provided irresistible invitations to join the literacy club, as Frank Smith (1988) called becoming a reader and writer. After a limited response initially to the call for family stories, children listened to their peers' family stories and wanted to join the parade. They went home and begged their parents for their stories. Family members, thus enticed, entered the procession with creativity and a glorious lack of uniformity.

Cambourne's second condition for engagement was that learners see the purposes of literacy for their lives. Personal and professional literacy was important to us as teachers, and to parents and other family members in a variety of ways. Children saw adults at home and school write to share information, build relationships, and gain new perspectives (e.g., about a child's reading development). Adults at home and school read to enjoy language, discover new information, enter a story world, and learn about their cultural heritages and those of others. Family members tell stories over and over that carry some meaning for that family's history and definition. When those stories came into the classroom, they served a similar purpose. Writing, as Calkins (1991) reminded us, is life's work, not artificial school work. We learned that many of the families shared their family stories with other relatives, sometimes long distance over the phone, sometimes at family gatherings. Cathy's mother said they took theirs on vacation, and laughed and cried together at the memories.

A third condition is that learners see the risks as low enough to chance engagement. We created a low-risk stance in several ways. Journals and stories were not graded. There was no single right way for adults or children to respond. We accepted and empathized wholeheartedly with family emergencies and conflicts, yet let parents know we believed they would again become involved after the emergency had passed.

Finally, learners have to have a bond with other doers. Families and teachers created a bond through journals as important co-teachers for the child; they appreciated each other, constantly writing supportive statements such as, "You are *doing* a great job teaching my child," and "What you *do* when you read with your child is so important!" Writing in journals and storytelling build on the strongest of bonds, those within families. Parents are children's first teachers, but school too often displaces parents from their teaching role. Parental help gets discounted with "my teacher said." Our parent-teacher-child journals encouraged the families to continue their teaching roles and showed the children that we as teachers respected parental teaching.

Now that we've looked at some of the complexities of engagement, we close with one mother's description. Mary, LaToya's mom, wrote about reading *Runaway Slave* together. "The book was kinda long but everytime we put it down we want to pick it back up to find out the ending. . . ." Mary and LaToya were indeed engaged readers. And, significantly we believe, their engagement with the book was enhanced by the extended community of parent, teacher, and child.

Extending the literacy community

There are more people in our literacy community now that we have opened doors to families and they have opened theirs to us. As Donald Graves (personal communication) said when we described parallel practices, "You've torn down walls between schools and homes." He commented on the effect we would have not only on the children in our classroom but on *their* children, since they were likely to become parents who valued and enjoyed shared reading and writing experiences. Parents commented on the impact of family storybook reading on siblings, who were often involved either as readers or listeners. According to social network theory, the more people a child interacts with around literacy, the more the child's literacy development will be facilitated (Baker et al., in press). Our students read and wrote with a variety or friends and family members.

The elements of reciprocity and respect were essential in establishing these extended communities. Cathy's mom told us that initially, when asked to "tell me about your child," she was worried about Betty's expectations. She quickly added, "But by the end of the second grade, I felt comfortable saying exactly what was on my mind." In discussing how teachers use authority to empower rather than control, Peterson (1992) wrote about teachers and students; however, we found his words to be just as true in considering interactions between teachers and family members: "Students [parents, and teachers] who are empowered have the *personal* authority needed to express themselves confidently, judge their work and the work of others, and take action in their own best interests as well as in the interest of others" (p. 119). Peterson singled out dialogue as an example, emphasizing that both participants must have control and responsibility, as all participants did in the home-school journals in our study. This authority, Peterson argued, is essential in building learning communities.

We learned about each other in new ways by connecting the communities of home and school. We are European American, middle-class women; our children were African American (70%) as well as European American, middle-class as well as struggling economically. We believed that what was most important about understanding our children was getting to know the individual family cultures, traditions, beliefs, and literacy experiences and standards rather than assuming a monolithic culture for all African American children, children living in poverty, and so on. Moll et al. (1992) noted that when teachers got to know families in their homes they fractured commonly held stereotypes. They learned that parents cared very much about their children's schooling and that they had strong philosophies of child rearing and of education; further, they learned the *specific* "funds of knowledge" within each household (e.g., knowledge of carpentry, farming, midwifery, child care). Similarly, the work of Denny Taylor and colleagues (e.g., Taylor and Strickland 1989; Taylor and Dorsey-Gaines, 1988) has shown widely different literacy experiences and purposes, even among families that may be demographically similar. Meetings with families, journals, and family stories were avenues that simultaneously built community and fostered two-way, individual understanding.

Peterson (1992) wrote that the most important discovery he ever made about teaching was that "community in itself is more important to learning than any method or technique" (p. 2). He was talking about the "crowded place" of the classroom; we extended community beyond classroom walls. Peterson described the link between community and learning:

> [Learning] has to do with our desire to make sense of our experience, to join with others, to become a part of a community. It has to do with developing our expressive abilities and participating in everything that interests us, with being able to benefit from the insight and experience of others . . . , with living and learning in a place outfitted with opportunities to learn, a place where we can fumble and make mistakes without being scorned or laughed at. (p. 3)

This description of community serves us well as a summary of this chapter and as an invitation to the rest of the book. In it, we hope to show how teachers, families, and children joined with others to make sense of their experiences, developed expressive abilities, and became an extended family of readers and writers.

THREE
Creating Parallel Practices

Nancie Atwell, a widely published teacher-researcher, is also a parent. In *Side by Side* (1991), she wrote about what she and her husband, Toby, wish for their daughter, Anne:

> We hope for a teacher who will understand writing, reading and Anne: someone who will observe what she knows and needs to know next, how she learns, and what she loves, someone who will speak to us of our daughter's literacy with passion and insight, someone so thoughtful about teaching and learning that when we visit Anne's classroom there isn't a program in sight. We dream of the thoughtful practices of a teacher researcher. (p. 16)

We, like Nancie and Toby, have dreamed this dream for our own children. We have rejoiced in every teacher who has taken a personal interest in our children. Each of us strives to be this kind of teacher, but we know we cannot do it well without the children's first teachers, their parents.

Betty and Barbara, as whole language teachers, base their instructional decisions on principles of meaningfulness, time, choice, community, responsibility, and social interaction. Children in their classrooms choose what they read, what they write about, what investigations they conduct, who they learn with, and many other aspects of self-regulated, experiential learning, elements that typify much of children's out-of-school learning. However, Betty and Barbara wanted to create a closer link between children's home lives and school lives. Along with this interest was a dissatisfaction with their previous use of homework, which had varied from none to occasional practice work that children could do independently. One of the first concerns parents have each year is homework. First graders and their parents think of homework as a milestone in their school experience and are excited to take home this marker of "real" school; predictably, however, that excitement usually lasts about a week. Betty and Barbara wanted to create homework that could sustain the interest of students, parents, and teachers all year long. The children's days in the classroom were filled with meaningful, relational literacy experiences. Could the experiences of home become integrated into the classroom community in a complementary way?

In their ground-breaking book *Women's Ways of Knowing*, Belenky, Clinchy, Goldberger, and Tarule (1986) discussed what they came to view as distinctly different ways of accessing knowledge: "separate knowers" and "connected knowers." According to their research, "Connected knowers develop procedures for gaining access to other people's knowledge. At the heart of these procedures is the capacity for empathy" (p. 113). These connected knowers' "purpose is not to judge but to understand"

Parallel Practices

At School	At Home
	Tell me about your child
	Parents inform teachers
	Home reading journals
We read every day	They read every night
Child chooses book	Child chooses book
We talk about books	They talk about books
Write what they chose	Write what they chose
	Family stories
Tell family stories ("Y'all know what?")	Tell family stories
Write family stories	Write family stories
Write memorable events	Parents write about own childhood
	Family reflection
Child reflects on how he or she learned to read and write	Families reflect on how child learned to read and write
Child writes evaluation of first grade	Parents write evaluation of first grade
Child writes expectation for second grade	Parents write expectation for second grade
	Adult literacy conversation
	Parents and teachers meet to talk about books and children

FIG. 3-1   *Parallel Practices*

(p. 116). As connected teachers, Betty and Barbara sought to understand, to connect with, both students and families. They trusted their students' thinking and encouraged them to expand it.

In response to her concerns and beliefs, Betty developed a set of parallel practices to link home and school (see Figure 3-1). Barbara strengthened the connection by continuing with the same group, adapting the practices based on feedback from parents and students. Betty and Barbara also decided to study the process, and they invited their long-time co-researcher, JoBeth, to participate. Parents became partners in the inquiry as they dialogued with Betty and Barbara in home journals and monthly meetings.

Tell me about your child

Each teacher issued an open-ended invitation to parents at the beginning of the year, similar to letters written by New York teachers in Calkins' *Living Between the Lines* (1991). Betty wrote, "Hello! Welcome to first grade! Parents have homework first! Please write and tell me about your child." Barbara wrote, "Dear Parents, It's always exciting to start a new school year with a new group of students. I look forward to working with your child. Please take a few moments to tell me about your child. Thanks, Barbara Michalove." Every parent, both years, wrote back. They shared how very special each child was in his or her family, as you will read in the Family Portraits section. They shared tips ("Torry's confidence in himself is not the greatest. However, he will overcome this with love and attention") and talents ("Ashley can find anything around the house and make it into something beautiful and interesting"), information about illnesses and family situations, and most of all, the love they have for these special children.

Home reading journals

Reading together and talking about books was the heart of the homework Betty and Barbara designed. Families somehow, amid difficult schedules, hardships, celebrations, and the everyday hassle of life, found time to enjoy literature together. As one child told Betty, "My mom read part of the first chapter of *Little House [on the Prairie]* while I was taking a bath. Yeah, I was in the tub and she was sitting on the toilet—the lid was down—and reading to me."

Just as they chose what books they would read at school, children chose books from the classroom library to take home with them each night. Three school nights each week in first grade, and two nights in second grade, children and families had homework. The families were encouraged through a letter (see Figure 3-2) to spend time together reading, talking, and writing about books. The child could read, another family member could read to the child, or they could read together; each family developed its own pattern based on its needs. Then they were encouraged to engage in a natural conversation about the book and to record their responses to the book in a journal.

The journal was a spiral notebook, inexpensive and easily replaced when full. The book and the journal traveled back and forth in a zip-top plastic bag. Betty and Barbara read journals during their half-hour planning period and responded to each individually. Some of the responses were only a sentence or two, and others were quite lengthy, but the personal responses were very important to children and other family members. LaToya's mother told Betty, "She comes home with the journal and starts asking me, 'What did she say? What did she say?' " Adam's mom remarked, "When you write those notes back, everybody runs to see what you said to them!"

Each family developed its own uses for the journal, including talking about books, illustrating, sharing information about the child's literacy development, occasionally conducting business, and sharing concerns (see Shockley [1993] for a discussion of

---

HOMEWORK . . . In our class, reading and writing are viewed as very connected and natural skills to learn. We read many books each day and write like real writers every day. Our homework practices also reflect this style of learning. Each night (except Friday) your child will bring a book and a reading journal home. Later in the year there will also be some spelling homework. For now, please read WITH your child every night. Remember, your child will be choosing the book s/he takes home, so on occasion the book may be too difficult for your child to read independently. You can help by asking your child if she wants to read the book herself or if she'd rather you read it to her. Then use the journal to write down her responses to the reading. Sometimes YOU may want to write me about the selection yourself and model for your child ways to think about what we read, or sometimes you may want to have your child dictate to you his interpretations, or sometimes your child may want to do it all by himself. What I'm trying to say is, relax—enjoy this time together—there's no one right way. . . .

FIG. 3-2   *Excerpt from Letter to Parents*

these uses). Rich examples from the journals are presented throughout this text, including a complete journal in Appendix A. We did not provide initial models of how to respond, nor did we have a particular academic agenda for our responses; rather, we wanted each family to construct a functional format and ways of dialoguing that were personally meaningful. Also, we wanted our writing to be responsive to the issues and ideas the families raised. Moll and colleagues (1992) pointed to reciprocity between families and school as a critical element in establishing enduring relationships. Our relationships with each family grew with every journal exchange. According to Moll et al., "reciprocal practices establish serious obligations based on the assumption of mutual trust, which is reestablished or confirmed with each exchange, and leads to the development of long-term relationships" (p. 134). When this kind of shared practice is present, "children have ample opportunities to participate in activities with people they trust."

Oral and written family stories

Betty had a storytelling time every day, a dependable opportunity for children to bring their home lives to school. She provided a storytelling stool and a battery-operated microphone, and the kids did the rest. A first-day volunteer, Kimberly, perched on the stool, legs swinging, shy but excited about a story she had to share. "Y'all know what?" she opened, and the group instinctively came to attention and chorused, "What?" On the second day, she used the same "call to story," and a year-long routine was born, copied from that day forth by every storyteller, including Ms. Shockley. Peterson (1992) described this kind of established and comfortable practice as a community ritual. "Ritual is a way of connecting to a larger community. It is more than talk. It is made up of symbolic acts that ground family and community life." Everyone knew there would be a time each morning to bring their homes to school through story and that a simple question could set in motion events that would become a part of that community's day and year as shared texts. Ritualistic calls to story and storytelling routines are a part of many cultures. As Belenky et al. (1986) note, "The connected class provides a culture for growth—as Elbow . . . says, a 'yogurt' class, as opposed to a 'movie' class (in which students are spectators)."

"Y'all know what" was a morning routine that was both predictable and surprising. The children could count on being able to narrate stories about their lives in the presence of a caring community, but often even the tellers were surprised by the responses they received. Rick told "fantastic" stories. Once, when he recounted an adventure at his apartment complex pool, it became obvious to all of us that he was telling some whoppers. After he told about jumping off his roof into the water, we talked about how sometimes it is fun and interesting to embellish stories to make the ordinary seem grander and that there were books in the classroom in which other storytellers had chosen to do the same thing, and that the name for that kind of story was a tall tale. After several other children attempted to cast their experiences in the same exaggerated form as Rick's, we read some tall tales and after lunch saw a video of *Pecos Bill*. Learning to touch reality with the fantastic became a goal for many of these young writers.

Families, all families, tell stories—some mundane, some historical, some to define themselves as a family. The children in both classrooms wrote every day in writing workshop (Calkins, 1986), again often sharing stories of their lives. It seemed another natural extension to ask parents to contribute a family story. They had already shown their willingness to be participants as they had written pieces telling about their children at the beginning of the year, and they had consistently been partners in dialogue with Betty in the response journals. Betty issued an open invitation to parents to write and share a family story with the class and to have their contribution included in a class book that would be available for the students to read as often as they liked. The invitation was open-ended, and each family wrote something different, from narratives about marriage, birth, death, and religion to poetry and family sayings ("If you kill a frog you will stump your toe.")

By second grade the children were confident about their families' desire and ability to participate. After a class discussion they decided unanimously that they wanted their parents to write about their own childhoods. Both child and parent (or other family member) contributed to this themed issue of *Stories from Our Lives* (1992). Ashley wrote about being attacked by a bulldog, and her mother reminisced about a tire swing in the family oak tree. Greg wrote about a ride at Disneyland; his aunt wrote about moving from California to Georgia. Barbara shared a Hanukkah memory, and Frances Ward, the instructional aide, told of swallowing a marble as her mother quilted nearby.

Lakendra reminded us that readers and writers need an audience when she wrote, "I love them when they lisn to me." Both classes published their family stories, and the children spent many days reading about one another's families and seeing in a concrete and shared way that even mothers and fathers, aunts, and grandparents experience, need, and use story. By modeling their lives and their efforts for the children, they added to the literacy legacies of both the home and school communities. We can only wonder at the family scenes when the writing was in process. Were there laughter in the remembering, worry over the rendering in print, discussions about spelling, grammar?

Betty invited these authors to a book reading and signing, which children and parents enjoyed immensely. Parents also read or had someone else read their second-year stories at one of the parent meetings. The literate community was indeed expanding.

Learning albums: family, child, teacher reflections

Reflecting on their own growth as readers and writers is arguably the most important form of evaluation for learners (Hansen, 1989). Evaluation by close members of their literate community provides a valuable second lens. At the end of each year Betty (Figure 3-3) and Barbara (Figure 3-4) asked children and parents to reflect on the children's literacy learning in a set of parallel questions. Parents wrote at home and were asked not to ask their children's opinion until after they gave their own; children wrote their reflections in school, where teachers could discuss responses with them.

Through this process, children had the opportunity to think about themselves as readers and writers, parents reflected on their children's development and on their expectations for the coming year, and Betty and Barbara gained valuable insights about children, families, and their own teaching. From reading the first-grade reflections, Barbara learned that most of the children and parents valued the reading and writing homework, so she decided to incorporate it in her own parallel practices. She also began the year with a good sense of what the children thought about themselves as readers and writers.

Parent Homework 1
Can your child read?
Does your child seem to enjoy reading?
How did your child learn to read? (Please
　answer this question based on what you
　think. Don't ask your child.)

Parent Homework 2
Can your child write?
Does your child like to write?
How do you think your child learned to write?
What do good first-grade writers know how
　to do?

Parent Homework 3
Tell me about your child now that he/she has
　finished first grade.
What's his/her outlook on learning?
How does she/he feel about school?
Was first grade a good experience?
What would you like his/her second-grade
　teacher to do for your child next year?
Are there things you hope to see continued?
Things that you hope will be done
　differently?
Do you have any advice?

Student Reflection
Can you read?
Do you like to read?
How did you learn to read?
How would you help someone else learn
　to read?
What were some of your favorite books
　you read this year?

Student Reflection
Can you write?
Do you like to write?
How did you learn to write?
How would you help someone else learn
　to write?

Student Reflection
What did you like about first grade?

What didn't you like about first grade?
What do you hope second grade will be.
　like?

FIG. 3-3　*First-grade End-of-year Reflections*

Parent Homework 1
Does your child seem to enjoy reading?
Does your child choose to read?
How do *you* think your child has developed
　this year as a reader?

Parent Homework 2
Does your child like to write?
Does your child choose to write at home?
How do *you* think your child has developed as
　a writer this year?
What do good second-grade writers know how
　to do?

Parent Homework 3
Tell me about your child now that he/she has
　finished second grade.
What's his/her outlook on learning?
How does he/she feel about school?
Was second grade a good experience?
What were some highlights of second grade for
　your child?
What would you like his/her third-grade
　teacher to do for your child next year?
Are there things you hope to see continued?
Things you hope will be done differently?
Do you have any advice?

Student Reflection
Do you like to read?
How did you get to be a better reader?
How would you help someone else learn to
　read?

Student Reflection
Do you like to write?
How did you get to be a better writer?
How would you help someone else learn to
　write?

Student Reflection
What did you like about second grade?

What didn't you like about second grade?
What hopes do you have about third grade?

FIG. 3-4　*Second-grade End-of-year Reflections*

Barbara learned from the children that the only thing they didn't like about first grade was "time out" for disruptive behavior, a practice she also employed. So when the next year began, she told the students she had read their concerns ("I love it when they lisn") and that this year there would be no time out. They would decide on the rules together, have a conference with Ms. Michalove or Ms. Ward to discuss the problem, and come up with a plan for the future. Now, truth be told, there were a few times during the year when a short cooling-off period in another classroom seemed necessary for a student, but for the most part class meetings and individual counseling sessions proved very successful.

These student and parent end-of-year reflections were a collection of learning snapshots we gathered throughout the two years of the study. These portraits of individual growth and change were catalogued in individual student notebooks, creating learning albums that informed both teachers and parents. The contributing "photographers" were from both home and school, creating different backdrops and perspectives. In the albums Betty and Barbara chronicled the literacy development of the students in a variety of poses, compositions, and time frames.

Learning albums, the collection of assessments, information, and reflections, were not portfolios (the children did not design or use them) but were a way for us to observe, study, and share growth over time. Included in the learning albums were student-parent reflections, "tell me about your child" letters, and photocopies of the response journals. Parents participated as co-evaluators; Betty sent home questions about areas of learning that had been addressed during specific units in science. Parents first explored answers with their child at home, allowing Betty to clarify any confusion through personalized teacher-child conversations the next school day. In addition, there were representative samples of student writing on self-selected topics as well as writing in which the students were asked to respond to a given topic for a prescribed amount of time. The three examples of this standardized sampling were collected over the school year, and visually (by length) and contextually (through story development) represented for teachers and parents student growth as writers.

Sharing informal reading inventories (IRIs) with parents during conferences also offered a quick visual path to understanding. These inventories were done at the beginning, middle, and end of the year. We graphed word recognition to show at a glance the growth patterns of individual learners; mapped with Marie Clay's timed ten-minute word-writing task, an individualized picture of word-level reading progress came into focus. We annotated the IRIs regarding understanding of various kinds of texts, reading mannerisms, and specific reading strategies. Response journals, of course, added to the emerging literacy profile of each child. Through our three-way partnership, all partners were able to contribute to and learn from these "big picture" albums of growth.

Parent meetings: adult literacy conversations

We invited the group of parents and other caretakers whose children were going into their second year together to meet with us throughout the year. We wanted to learn from the families what they thought was important about literacy and schooling, and we wanted them to have a forum for making decisions about their children's school year. Parents decided that the school was the most convenient meeting location and that free child care was a must. We hired Ms. Elder, the instructional aide who worked with Betty, and her daughters Thomasina and Simone, to provide this service.

We held seven meetings during the year. At the first, on September 3, eight mothers, four fathers, and assorted students and siblings (this was before we had set up child care) gathered in Barbara's room from 7 to 8 p.m. Betty read an article that she had written about the home journals and family stories the previous year (Shockley 1993) to ask for feedback before it was published; each family was represented somewhere in the article, using their real names (at their request). She got applause, misty eyes, and a letter from Brandon's mother that made its way into the article (see end of this chapter). Betty then passed the torch (and the children) to Barbara, who led parents in a discussion of how they wanted to structure the homework this year. They were very enthusiastic about this opportunity to "do things together," "interact," "communicate with the teacher all the time, not just at conferences," and to structure time together during their busy lives. They decided to keep the format the same but to write in the journals two nights a week rather than three, with children still reading and discussing books with their parents on the other nights.

Barbara explained that the class had generated a list of what the kids wanted to learn and do during the year; this would become a major part of their curriculum. The list included going camping, hiking, and fishing; studying Australia; going on a dinosaur dig; learning about various animals; going to the zoo and a ballet; and visiting a soft drink factory. Parents then gave their own interests and ideas, including studying geography, going on the camping trip, and "going to Australia—take me too!" Eight parents did attend all or part of the class campout in October.

The next parent meeting focused on family memories. Betty read excerpts from several books that told family stories, including *The Hundred Penny Box* by Sharon Bell Mathis, and invited parents to share their memories. Parents and teachers talked, laughed, and remembered. This discussion led many parents into their contribution to the *Stories of Our Lives,* which they wrote over the next few weeks.

In December about half the parents gathered to assemble these stories into books. We sewed pages together, then glued them into "marbled" covers the children had made using oil paints and water on glossy paper over cardboard. As we worked, some parents shared the stories they had written; most asked that Betty or Barbara read them aloud, which we did.

At the February meeting we shared books. Four of the eight parents and the three of us brought adult books we had been reading and briefly shared them. Then Barbara remarked on how many of the children in class were making the transition to short chapter books, and others would be following soon. She talked about a dozen books in this category, including popular mysteries, the Boxcar Children series (e.g., Warner, 1950; 1961), and the Stories Julian Tells series (e.g., Cameron, 1981).

Parents had each gotten a copy of Betty's published article. Brad's mom, Pam, said, "I was so excited about the family stories, and our little excerpts from the article—I *had* to talk to someone, so I called my relatives. I almost cried when I read Brandon's mom saying she finally realized she's a good mom." Others said they often reread the article and shared it with friends. We issued an invitation to present with us at the Children's Literature Conference, and three mothers indicated an interest (Colin's mom did present with us).

As we were leaving that night, Greg's Aunt Debra, newly stationed in Athens and new to motherhood, showed us that our hope of creating an extended community was becoming a reality. "You know what would be really fun?" she asked. "An overnight campout for *us,* not the kids, just us women. Build a fire, drink hot chocolate, and just talk."

At our May meeting we asked parents to share their thoughts about this year and their hopes for next year with us. They talked about having the kids stay together as a group; parents thought it had been beneficial, that the children had gotten to know each other "like brothers and sisters" and had learned how to work together. Everyone mentioned how much they enjoyed the books, whether they read them or their children read them. Parents talked in very specific ways about how much their children had grown as both readers and writers. In thinking about third grade, they wanted to continue the reading, and they wanted their children to continue to have a voice in creating the curriculum and to have fun with their learning.

The last event of the year was a family picnic at a city park, with fourteen of eighteen families attending. The year had come full circle, for once again the children, parents, siblings, and teachers were together.

Parental approval

Parental approval isn't a signed permission form. For us, it came about through a year-long process of oral and written dialogue.

At the end of the second-grade year, during the May parent meeting, we asked family members to talk about what difference, if any, these home-school experiences had made. Much of the conversation concerned the journals. Kate said, "I think it's a very good start, you know, to start that early, to be able to say that—okay, things are going on with me and I'm going to write them down here and I can kinda see what's going on, you know, thinking and seeing it on paper." Debbie added that it gave her a way to watch Adrian grow: "Their thinking grows from the beginning of the school year, the way they were writing and to where they are putting their concepts together . . . I saw a major difference even from the beginning of this school year—he's really wanting to think about what he's saying instead of copying it directly from the book."

Another mother pointed out that what really kept her daughter interested was "a response from the teacher." They were most appreciative of the time Betty and Barbara spent responding in a personal, positive way to each entry. "It wasn't just 'you did good,' you know, 'keep up the good work.' " They also liked having the communication channel with the teacher. Susan told Barbara, "I really feel closer to you as a teacher than I did when Charlie was in [your room] . . . we kinda feel like family." Debbie agreed: "You're human now. [Before] we only saw you as a teacher."

To a person, these family members said that the opportunities to be actively involved with their children's reading and writing, and with their children's teachers, were very important to them; but nobody said it better than Brandon's mother, Kathryn:*

---

*As a general rule, we have printed all excerpts from journals and family stories as they were shared with us and as we shared them with families. (One parent did edit her own writing in several places, and we have honored her edits.) We made careless errors, as did family members, and we have included those along with the writings of parents who did not employ all the conventions of edited English, because we want our examples to be real, for readers to see that it was the process, not the product, that engaged us.

Ms. Shockley,

When you said that we were a "special group because of the 100% participation", I felt proud but at the same time a little shocked and a little sad.

When I grew up, it was hard for me to get my parents to participate in anything I did in school. That really affected my sense of "worth". I thought I was a burden to my parents. Also, I wasn't really excited about school. I felt if my parents didn't care, why should I? That is why I take the time out with Brandon in helping him with his school work. I want him to get excited about homework.

I was so glad for the "homework". It gave me the opportunity to be in the "scholastic" part of his learning. I can appreciate it and I feel that it has helped Brandon's learning. I remember when the journals first started I would read to Brandon. Towards the end Brandon read to me. He was eager to learn more words so that he could read more, so he learned!

I think my child is special. I have only one time to raise him and one time to teach him and one time to be a part of his growing up. If I show I care, then maybe he would be that caring parent also.

Kathryn Eberhart

FAMILY
PORTRAITS

FOUR
Adrian: The Moral of the Story

Our son, Adrian Jerome Anderson, is the highlight of our life. He's very outgoing. He plays well with others. He's interested in learning and willing to try new things. He's very independent, attentive, and gregarious.

Adrian is very obedient. He has been taught to respect others and obey grown-ups, but occasionally he tries to see how far he can go over the line. A mere reminder is all he needs to put him back on the right track.

Adrian is an only child, but he does not possess the characteristics of an only child. Adrian likes music, books, remote control cars, Ninja Turtles, GI Joes, and Martial Arts. His favorite foods are pizza, french fries, broccoli, rice, hot dogs, and pork chops.

The best thing about Adrian is he is a very warm and lovable person. His father and I love him very much and he knows it. We hope this sounds like the writings of proud parents, because we are very proud of Adrian. If we had to describe Adrian with one word, that word would be special because that's what he is to us.

Mr. and Mrs. Jerry Anderson

Sharing information, teacher-to-teacher

The love that Adrian's parents expressed as they introduced their son to his new teachers permeated the home-school connection they (especially his mother, Debbie) formed first with Betty, then with Barbara. They developed a mutual admiration society that was based on genuine love and concern over Adrian and his development, and appreciation of the efforts of each in his interest. They informed each other throughout the year about how he was developing as a reader, writer, and thoughtful human being.

Debbie's observation that Adrian was "interested in learning" was evident in his first book choice, *Science,* the Addison-Wesley first-grade textbook Betty displayed alongside the hundreds of trade books in her classroom library. What a novel way to look at curriculum—textbooks so appealing that kids choose to take them home and actually read them. Of course, in this case, Debbie read the book to Adrian, half of it the first night, the other half the second. They used the journal to record what Adrian learned about plants and animals, and for Adrian to illustrate "the experiment we did from lesson two" (9/18).

The next night Adrian lugged home *Bears of the World* (Domico, 1988), which could have been a textbook for a course Bears 101. Debbie apologized, saying that

---

This introduction is a blend of the two different letters the Andersons wrote at beginning of the first and second grades when each teacher asked, "Tell me about your child."

"because we didn't get home until 6:45, we were not able to go into great detail with the book"; however, "Adrian was most intrigued by the fact that bears can run up to 40 miles per hour for a short distance. We used the speed limit on North Avenue to compare the rate of speed of the bears" (9/23). This was indicative of the active involvement the two of them had with books throughout the first and second grades. Together, they read and wrote about amazing animals, medieval castles, and the animals of Australia as well as many fables, fairy tales, and funny stories.

Betty got a strong sense from these first few journal entries that Debbie knew she was an important teacher in her son's life. After several supportive statements about their learning together, Betty asked Debbie a question. Debbie responded with a personal note, beginning "Mrs. Shockley." It was interesting that she addressed this to Betty personally, when all the previous entries (and those for the rest of the year) had obviously been to Betty but without any form of address. This seemed to establish a personal relationship between the two adults that became a year-long conversation including talk about books, talk about Adrian, and talk about life's incidental but important events, such as a birthday party.

There is a level of intimacy established in the journals that makes reading them feel like eavesdropping on a conversation. Many entries are a true dialogue (this was not always the case, as many parents and children focused so much on writing the response to the book that they ignored questions from the teacher). The following excerpts from September to December provide a glimpse into this intimate conversation:

Debbie: Adrian and I read the book when we got home, however, because yesterday was so busy we didn't have time to discuss the book. Please excuse us this time. (9/91)

Betty: You are most certainly excused! I hope you had a great birthday celebration.

Debbie: Thank you! We did indeed have a great time.

Debbie: . . . We read Paul Bunyan together and I'm pleased with the progress Adrian is making. (11/91)

Betty: Adrian sets such big goals for himself. Let me know if he shows signs of becoming frustrated. I haven't noticed that he is here.

Debbie: I have not noticed frustration; only disappointment. He needs at least 6 more hours in the day to accomplish all the things he has decided he *has* to do. . . . He's decided he wants to be a kindergarten teacher. . . .

Debbie: . . . Books like this one reminds me of my own childhood. When books were written solely for entertainment and not profit. (12/91)

Betty: What a wonderful connection for you—Did you talk with Adrian about your feelings?

Debbie: Yes. He found it hard to believe we had books that long ago!

Betty: Wow—Only from a child—right?

In January, Debbie told Betty about a mild reprimand she had given her son.

Debbie: . . . Tell me if you think I'm being too hard on him, I'm also learning as we go. . . .

Betty: Fortunately, I feel like I'm always learning too. . . . You do know your son very well, however. . . . It is wonderful to have a student who *always* seems to be interested in *everything*—what a treasure he is!

Debbie: Thank you! And you are a delight to work with. . . .

How often do we as parents have someone to talk over our decisions with, to tell us how well we are raising our children? How often as teachers do we have someone tell us how well we are teaching, and talk with us teacher-to-teacher?

In March, Adrian began writing many of his own responses; occasionally Debbie added a message of her own. She continued this pattern in second grade. Adrian wrote the first entry, Barbara asked him questions, and Debbie wrote:

> Thank you for asking the questions above. I too asked Adrian the same question. . . . I knew that if your teaching standards were like Ms. Shockley's you would catch this. . . . He will start putting more time in his writing. . . .

Perhaps because the home-school connection had been maintained, perhaps because Betty "handed over" her intact class to Barbara during the first parent meeting, Debbie continued the conversation she had begun the previous year. When she responded to *The Spaceship,* Debbie wrote, "What an interesting book. It seems like this kid has a vivid imagination. I believe our kids could write a story of the same caliber." Not only had she shared her son with his teachers, she shared with them the pride in the whole class—*our* kids.

When Adrian did not return to class after the winter holiday, Barbara wrote:

Barbara: We missed you on Monday. I was a little worried that you moved away during the holidays. I sure was glad to see you on Tuesday!

Debbie: We are glad to be back. I missed writing in and reading the Journal. Adrian was glad to get back to school and see all of his friends. Everyone at home knows all about Ms. Michalove and her 2nd grade class. We have some fun memories and good friends at Fowler. We could never leave without saying goodbye. Adrian was excited about the new books the class received. Midieval castles peeked new interests.

While it did not happen overnight, Adrian eventually engaged in the same kind of dialogue his mother and teachers had so enjoyed. In March of second grade the following exchange took place over the course of a week:

Adrian: Kitman and Willy This is a funny story. The best part was when Kitman pulled down the moon.

Barbara: Adrian—you like funny stories, don't you? Have you ever tried to write a funny story?

Adrian: No have you Goldilocks And The three bears Mr. Marshall really used his imagination. I think that's cool I will write a funny story one day

Barbara: I know you will, Adrian! You can do anything you want if you work hard enough. I think reading a lot of funny stories will help you write your story. I have not written a funny story . . . well, maybe one. Last year this girl, Jamie, in our class got her arm stuck in the table. What happened was totally ridiculous. I laughed and laughed. Then I wrote a funny song about it. I'm pretty good at writing stories with surprise endings but not too great at funny stories. I need to practice. Ms. M.

Much of what educators have learned recently about emergent literacy has come from studying parent-child interaction. For example, parents reading with their children usually scaffold the interaction over time, providing just enough support for the child to become increasingly independent (Yaden, Smolkin, and Conlon, 1989). Building the scaffold (finding the right balance between independence and support) is an interactive process, where parent and child contribute, suggest, offer, and read the signals the other is giving. Debbie was very effective in following her son's signals and at times suggesting increased independence a bit ahead of his signals. She seemed to understand Lisa Delpit's (1991) point that "instruction can be both child-centered and teacher-directed at the same time. The child-centeredness comes with understanding what the child needs at any given moment" (p. 547).

With Debbie, as with the other parents, we did not explain scaffolding; that would have been inappropriate in an equal relationship where we were interested in learning how parents thought their children should learn, and it would have been unnecessary as well. Most were working so closely and so consistently with their children that they came to understand "what the child needs" and provided support.

As Adrian became increasingly interested in and capable of reading to himself or his mother and writing his own responses, Debbie helped us address the question of what parents can do when their children become independent readers and writers. Several times, Debbie informed Betty or Barbara of some shift in the parent-child reading-writing format. For example, in November of first grade she wrote, "Adrian has reverse the reading role. He has begun to read by himself without asking me to do it for him. I think it's wonderful." In October of second grade she wrote Barbara that Adrian needed to write more about the story content and that she (Barbara) would see "more in depth writing in the future." She helped Adrian accomplish this by doing their response to *The Frog Prince, Continued* together, labeled "Mom's Part" and "Adrian's Part." She stayed involved, listening to him read and recording his responses. When he was doing almost all the reading and writing independently in second grade, they still discussed the books, and she helped him correct his entries.

Family values

Adrian and his parents really enjoyed the literature they read together. They delighted in its language and cleverness, learned from it about science and history, and grew attached to favorite authors like Leonard Kessler, James Marshall, and Steven Kellogg. However, Debbie saw literature as more than information and entertainment; she used it as a vehicle for discussing and teaching the family's moral values to Adrian. She frequently asked Adrian to verbalize the moral of a story, and in the process they engaged in personalized, interpretive discussions.

Debbie introduced the "moral of the story" in September of first grade when she and Adrian read *Arthur's Eyes* (Brown, 1979): "We (Adrian) learned that glasses are very important to people (Particularly his mom). And that you shouldn't laugh or make fun of people because their appearance is different." A week later she explicitly taught him, in their discussion of *Chicken Little* (Kellogg, 1985):

> After reading the story we discussed what morals of stories mean. The moral of the story from Adrian's point of view is don't believe someone is a policemen just because he has on a suit. He said, "A policemen has a gun, a badge and hand cuffs. And anyway the sky don't fall."

This may not have been exactly what she was looking for, but Debbie accepted his interpretation. The rest of the first-grade journal contains many "moral" lessons. Mother and son discussed taking care of other people's things, being polite when others are talking, and appropriate school behavior. *Goldilocks* led to the conclusion that children should listen to their parents. Adrian learned from *Fantastic Mr. Fox,* "No matter how bad things seem, if you stop and think you can usually find a solution to the problem." In April, Adrian and his mom read *Jack the Bum and the UFO* and decided that "Jack may not have a lot of material things, but he has a lot of heart."

Developing a sense of values continued as a topic of response in second grade. Debbie wrote about their discussion of *Galimoto:*

> This book shows what hard work and determination can do for you. I asked Adrian what he thought the moral of the story was and his response was "don't let someone tell you what you can't do."

Barbara wrote back:

> Good for you, Adrian. I think you're right, and be sure not to let anybody tell you that you can't do something that you know you can! I also liked the setting of this story. Last year we had a visitor from Somalia. . . . He told us all the children make galimotos out of odds and ends. . . .

Up to this point, Debbie had written all the "moral" interpretations; when Adrian wrote, it was usually "My favorite part was when . . ." However, at the end of October (second grade), Adrian wrote:

> In a Town There Was a young Boy who was a WoodCutter. He Saw that Town and Said he was not afraid of Nothing. The Morale of The Story is How Big you are Doesn't Mean the Bigger the Badest.

Adrian included one more moral the next month, then stopped. Apparently Debbie decided he needed more support in thinking deeply about stories, and connecting them to his life. Although Adrian had been writing almost all the entries for most of the year, Debbie wrote on January 19:

> Adrian and I read this book together. We've decided to take turns writing this [new calendar] year. We discussed the moral of the story and Adrian said never lie about something to get attention. He said that if you tell your parents you have a cold to stay home from school, the next time you're really sick they won't believe you.

Sure enough, soon after, when it was Adrian's turn, he wrote, "Little Red Riding Hood should have followed her mother's rules and She wouldn't have been in the wolf's stomach."

Family literacy standards

Adrian's mother had high standards for his writing as well as for his moral development. After Adrian completed an entry (with a great deal of help from Mom), Debbie wrote:

> I enjoyed listening to Adrian as he read this book. He fussed about writing the last assignment, so we agreed to alternate. I won't force him, but I think he should try every once in a while. (10/7, first grade)

Betty was very supportive of this decision:

> Dear Adrian, You did a great job writing about *Piggies*. I bet it's nice for your mom to write for you because you have so many ideas about what you read and it might seem too much to write it all down. Maybe you could write one thing and you could tell your mom the rest. What do you think? Love, Ms. Shockley

Debbie replied that Adrian "thought your idea was great." They did a couple of entries together, then Adrian stopped writing again for several months (although they always read and talked) and had Mom record a response.

Finally, in February of first grade Debbie wrote, "Adrian will start writing in his Journal next week. It seemed we could never sit down long enough for him to write. . . ." We realized it took much longer for Debbie to supervise, correct, and teach Adrian than it took to write things herself; but she had decided it was time for Adrian to write. Shortly after that, Adrian wrote, "Charles Tiger Its a nice book I apshl like the pach wethe the moke in it [I especially like the page with the monkey in it.]" Debbie wrote under his entry, "I started to correct his spelling but I decided to let you see his efforts. He's really trying!" Betty replied, "I'm so glad you didn't correct the spelling. We could read it just fine—*especially* those invented spellings. This is great!!!!!!!!!!"

Whether Debbie had seen school writing with invented spelling, or had just realized how much effort had gone into his attempt, we don't know; whatever the reason, Betty was obviously pleased. However, when Debbie tore a page out of the journal later in the year and had Adrian rewrite it "neater," Betty told him she was glad, because it made it easier for "others (like me) to read it." Betty felt it was important to let her students know how much she respected their parents as literacy teachers, even when their approaches were different.

By second grade Debbie was insisting on a lengthy, content-oriented response, written neatly and spelled correctly (for the most part). Barbara estimated that Adrian and his mom or dad spent about an hour reading and writing each night they had homework (two nights a week). Barbara was supportive of these expectations and complimented Adrian each time his responses improved in content or legibility. Toward the end of the year Adrian was an advanced phonemic speller in daily writing work-shops, but in the journal his mom insisted on correct spelling. Barbara got a glimpse of how strongly Debbie felt about this issue from Adrian's April 5 entry:

> The not so Jally roge I think that is't a cool Book becaues It's about 3 boys hows names were Joe Fred and Sam. He got a Book form His Okol Joe. fred wished He was in piret time and ther they were. they saw Black Berd and all that pirting they got back to new yow. finley.

This entry had a large X through it and "Disregard" written above it. Directly below was the following entry:

> The Not So Jolly Ranger I think is a cool book because it's about 3 boys whose name are Joe, fred and Sam. Joe got a book from his uncle about pirates, knights, castles and

other things. Fred wished they could live during the pirate time and there they were. They saw Black Beard and witness all that pirating. They got back to New York finally.

It's not perfect—she's not a fanatic about it—but it certainly is much more conventional than his first (unsupervised) draft. Adrian's mother wrote in her end-of-year reflection, "Good second[-grade] writers should know how to make complete sentences using correct grammar and punctuation. They should also be able to put their thoughts on paper." As Lisa Delpit (1991) put it:

> It is vital that everyone develop a sense of personal literacy—using literacy for entertainment, to further one's own thinking, to clarify one's emotions, to share with intimates, to keep track of important issues in one's life. But power code literacy [conventional, edited English] gives you access to the world outside of yourself and your immediate circle of intimates. (p. 543)

The Andersons were making sure that Adrian had both a love of literature and access to the code of power.

Neither Betty nor Barbara tried to "train the parent" to adopt school views of literacy in their home interactions; they shared their own beliefs at times and respected Debbie's choices. There were some conflicting priorities. Betty's first priority was for the time to be enjoyable, and it wasn't always for Adrian (he wants "no homework" in third grade); Mom wanted it to be enjoyable but it was first and foremost a learning time.

Although their expectations were sometimes different, Betty, Barbara, and Debbie all let Adrian know that they valued his writing, and this was evident in Adrian's end-of-first-grade reflections on reading and writing: "Whin i Was 1. I uos to write like chenkn strst [chicken scratch] And Whin I was 5. I latitorede [learned to read] And theer you havae it." And we do—he has two essential elements, invention and the influence of reading on writing. In his commentary on teaching someone else to write, he included a third element, encouragement of approximation: "I wood Farst tall them to do stnkn strach. And whin they DiD That OK you DiD a good job."

Adrian's dad, Jerry, was also involved in reading and writing with Adrian, although he had few opportunities because he was a sergeant in the army and was stationed overseas much of both years. When he was home on leave, Debbie wrote, "Adrian read to his father, but I got the pleasure of writing in the journal. The two are in high heaven now and I can sigh a big relief." In another entry, Dad recorded and illustrated Adrian's response. At the end of the year, he wrote one of the most extended reflections of any parent on first grade, and his hopes and expectations for Adrian's second-grade experience:

> We can see a definite change in Adrian. He has gone from dreading going to school to looking forward to the next day. . . . I'd like his teacher to continue to be creative like his first teachers were. I like the idea of learning outside of the textbook. Learning is fundamental, but it should also be fun. I especially liked the idea of bringing a different book home each night and a journal to write down ideas, concerns, or whatever was on your mind. . . . Continue to push for more parent involvement. Encourage a stronger parent-teacher relationship. I liked knowing what and how Adrian was doing in school all year long, not just at parent/teacher conference.

Debbie was active in the parent meetings during second grade; Jerry also came when he was in town. The first year Debbie wrote the family stories; in second grade Jerry contributed his own, hilarious childhood memory.

First-grade family story
Mommy, Where Did You Meet Daddy?
By Debbie Anderson, mother of Adrian Anderson*

Mommy, where did you meet daddy?

Well, your Dad and I were both in the Army in 1979. We were both stationed at Fort Polk, Louisiana.

Yeah, that's where Mrs. Barbara and Mr. Hank live.

We became good friends. After a year we realized we liked each other more than friends. We decided to get married and all of the wedding plans were made.

Then one week before the wedding we were sent on a secret mission (yeah, really secret. We couldn't tell anyone. I could only tell Grandmom we were leaving and we would miss the wedding.) to Fort Chaffee, Arkansas, to police the Cuban refugees.

What's a refugee?

It's a person who leaves his country to escape danger or hard times for a better way of life. We had to cancel our plans and we didn't know when we would get married.

Tell me more about those—uh, what kind of refugees?

Cuban. They are people from Cuba, and I thought you wanted to hear about your dad and me.

Oh, yeah. O.K.

Let's see, where was I? Oh, I know; well while we were in Arkansas I got orders to go to Germany, and since Dad and I were not married yet, he didn't get any orders. So on your Dad's birthday we had a small private wedding, and I left for Germany two weeks later.

Now that we were married your dad could join me in Germany. (No, you were not born then. I know you went to Germany, but that was our second trip.) Your dad got orders three months later and he joined me in Germany.

We stayed there for three years and then we moved to Alabama. (Right! That's where you were born.) We've been together for eleven years now. (Well, I know he's not here right now, but we're still together through letters and phone calls, and before you know, he'll be back.)

Now it's time to go to sleep. No, I'll have to tell you stories about Turkey some other time. Good night! I love you, too!

The next year when Barbara's class decided they wanted their parents to write about a childhood memory, Jerry Anderson was home and contributed the following story from his childhood (*Stories from Our Lives,* 1992):

Growing up on a farm was very exciting. Something new and exciting happened everyday. We had a lot of farm animals, but a particular hog stood out from all the rest. He was not like the other hogs. He acted as if he was always mad. He would never let you feed the other hogs because he would chase you if you came inside the fence. And he would always find a way to escape. He was too much trouble so my father decided to sell him.

---

*From *Family Stories* (1992). Debbie adopted the format of *Tell Me a Story, Mama,* by Angela Johnson, a story they had read at home, after a conversation with Betty about how she might write her story.

Mr. Shed was a blind man who lived on a nearby farm. He bought the hog from my father, but he couldn't get him home without help. My father told my brother and me to help Mr. Shed with his new hog. I had had some bad experiences with this hog and was not too eager to help.

We set out to catch this hog by putting a rope on his neck so we could put him on our truck. I explained my indifference about the hog to Mr. Shed, who didn't understand why a fourteen year old would be afraid of a simple farm animal. He told me to stand back, he would get the hog. Bare in mind that even though Mr. Shed was blind he could travel anywhere he wanted to without any help. He could travel day or night and never get lost.

He went into the pen followed by my brother and me. All of the other hogs ran inside their pen, except the mean one who immediately charged at us. I wanted to run, but I didn't want to leave Mr. Shed. I turned to see Mr. Shed swinging his cane wildly in the air hollering "Down hog! Down! Down!" My father heard the commotion and ran and rescued all of us. Mr. Shed was so shaken but he didn't want us to see it after the hard time he had given us for being afraid of a hog.

After it was all over my brother and I lay on the ground and laughed uncontrollably. Everytime we looked at each other we'd start swinging wildly and saying "Down hog! Down! Down!"

Literacy standards were not something abstract or simply imposed in Adrian's family. They were a part of their lives, and they were making sure that they would be a part of Adrian's life too.

Supported literacy development

Reading, writing, direct instruction, and connected literacy experiences supported breadth and depth in Adrian's literacy development. All three key parties in the teaching-learning triangle agreed, although each portrayed it differently.

According to Debbie, Adrian could both read and write, and liked to do so, by the end of first grade. She said he learned to read "with the help of flash cards [at home], book with cassette, and reading along with bedtime stories. But, his reading was enhanced by the books he brought home daily from school." He learned how to write from her teaching him his alphabet at home as well as from the writing he did in school. After second grade Debbie wrote that he "has matured as a reader. He's willing to finish a story on his own. He does not require a lot of coaching when he reads. He knows the type of books he likes to read and their authors, but he's willing to venture into other categories as well." As a writer: "I think Adrian has developed as an improved writer in his penmanship, his willingness to read more and think about what he has read and apply what he has read in his own thoughts on paper." Again, she valued the development of personal literacy—"to further one's own thinking"—as well as power code literacy (in this case, legibility).

Betty and Barbara heartily agreed with each of these thoughtful developmental markers. In addition, they had other kinds of information. At the beginning of first grade Adrian recognized and could write his letters and a few isolated words; he was not reading connected text. By January of that year he read 73 of 76 words correctly in a mid–Grade 1 graded passage. At the end of first grade he missed only two words on the 1+ passage, reading with expression and understanding. He read with similar proficiency on second-grade passages the next year. His writing progressed from a few _ conventionally spelled labels to several-page stories with detailed illustrations, using advanced phonemic and conventional spelling. His responses to literature grew in second grade to include half-page informational reports, moral-of-the-story, chapter by chapter reports, personal connection ("I which that was Dad and Me" to *How Many Stars in the Sky?*), and even a review: "When you read Wolverine you'll love it if you like action and excitement. I guarantee you'll love this book."

And what of Adrian himself? We've already heard his thoughts on how he became a writer. This is what he had to say about becoming a reader, a response that shows the home-school connection from his point of view:

When i was 5 My MoM. We ues'to go to The LiBarey Then When i got to fastgad [first grade] i Lade hay to reDy Book [learned how to read books].

FIVE

Lakendra: ". . . and as always we were pleased"

From the very beginning when Janice wrote about her child, Lakendra, the hope and strength in this mother-daughter relationship were apparent:

Lakendra Echols is very witty. She likes to go to movies, and she like to go to the mall especially the toy store. And most of all she likes to help with the house work. Washing dishes the most. Lakendra like to be my big girl; she's very out-spoken about what's she feel. Me and Lakendra have no secrets from each other. I can trust my big girl and she can count on me. She's my little star.

As this initial sharing gained dimension through journal exchanges, it became clear that Lakendra's mother took her role as parent seriously yet softly. She was always there ready to share her insights, consider new ideas, and support us all as we journeyed down a winding road to literacy. Janice saw herself as a teacher too, and rightfully so, but she was also ready and willing to be a learner—a stance we found important for all of us.

Joint construction of support

The first day in first grade that the journal went home, Janice and Lakendra used it for recording lists of words. This made perfect sense, given that the tablets Betty gave the students were clearly labeled by the manufacturer as being spelling tablets. No school-assigned spelling words had accompanied the journal home, but that didn't stop this duo. They dutifully reported on page 1: "These are some of the words me and Lakendra are studying." After Betty talked briefly with Lakendra the next morning about other ways the journal might be used, she and her mom established a lasting partnership with each other, their teachers, and books.

So, was that all it took? Books. A child. People who cared. A way to communicate. You would think with such a simple recipe the end result would be fairly predictable. Not so. Each family-child-teacher partnership evolved differently, developing unique response patterns that suited their particular needs and comfort levels. For instance, the journals co-authored by Janice, Lakendra, Betty, and Barbara are unlike any others; they are examples of a special reporting style that was initiated by Janice in support of her daughter's literacy development. Lakendra, her mother, and her teachers spent two years building literary bridges that really counted for something. We helped one another notice things. We gave one another pats on the back. We really cared.

By the second day of journal writing, a style was born. Janice settled into a pattern of reporting that continued to be reliable over time. She shared her observations of the successes and struggles that she and Lakendra experienced as they blended their knowledge about reading and writing with those of the classroom teachers. Her very active and reflective role in supporting Lakendra's progress provided an interactive sounding board for ideas to be exchanged, considered, and reconsidered. Sometimes we would all agree. Sometimes Janice or the classroom teacher would offer some additional information on an issue. In either case, there were trust, respect, and encouragement for everyone's efforts.

Betty and Barbara tried to match their response styles to those initiated by the families, consciously accepting and supporting the family's form and content. Janice and Lakendra designed their response journal to express the meaningfulness of the effort, their relationship, and Janice's pride in her daughter.

Early in first grade Janice wrote:

> Ms. Shockley, Lakendra chose Old MacDonald as her reading for last night. She started out singing the song Old MacDonald until I sit down with her and pointed it out word for word but she did good.

Betty, just learning herself what kind of support Lakendra needed, responded with a suggestion:

> You may want to let Lakendra do the book her way first then together you could get her to point *with* you to the words as you reread the story.

It wasn't long before Janice shared another idea with Betty by asking her opinion about getting longer books:

Janice: In the story I Can Fly Lakendra did very good. Her reading was very good. And maybe she's ready to move on to a few more words. I mean a book with a few more words. If you think so also. (9/30/91)

Betty: I agree. She can read more difficult books but like everybody, young readers enjoy reading things that are easy for them too.

Betty supported her suggestion both in the journal and by helping Lakendra find books with "a few more words." And so they continued day by day exploring together the possibilities of the reading process.

Janice: Ms. Shockley, In the story of the Halloween Performance, Lakendra seem to have some problems with many of the words. Maybe she get a story with too many difficult words for her right now. But still I enjoyed her reading. Thank You. Janice Barnett (10/2/91)

Betty: This is probably an example of one of those times Lakendra chose a book that it would be best for you just to read to her. When you get ready to read together each night, you might begin by asking Lakendra—Do you want to read your book to me or do you want me to read to you? Sometimes after you read even a more difficult book she may ask to read it after you. Let her be the leader. One of the most important things about sharing books together is talking about them together. Thanks.

Janice: Lakendra was very excited about the books she chose to read to me. So excited she read them over and over again. And I was so pleased. Maybe last night she did want me to read the story to her I don't know but I will ask her from now on. Because she was a little upset that she didn't know a lot of the words. And I don't ever want her to feel pressured. Thanks. Janice Barnett (10/3/91)

Later that first-grade year Janice wrote:

Janice: Ms. Shockley, I'm glad to see Lakendra is getting stories with a little more words and I can see she really tries even if she can't get them all right the words I mean. In the story Chicka Chicka Boom Boom she read the story but she didn't know all the words but at least she tried and when she finished I read her the story again and I think she really enjoyed it a little better. Thanks. Janice B.

Betty: I wonder how it would be if when she brings home a book that is a little too hard, you read it first and then let her try it. Let me know how that way works compared to her reading first. Thanks!

Janice: Ms. Shockley, Now that's a good idea I never thought of that but I will try it. In the story the Big Toe Lakendra did good and I enjoyed it the story left both of us asking the question of who's big toe was it? Thanks. Janice B.

At one point in first grade Janice raised a concern about sequencing. It was in response to Lakendra's reading of *Chicken Soup with Rice*. Since the sequence of that story depended on an understanding of the twelve months of the year, Betty did not pursue the issue in depth in her response; questions related to understanding texts did not appear again in the journal that year. Lakendra's end-of-first-grade informal reading inventory showed her reading at a 90 percent accuracy rate on a passage from an Arnold Lobel Frog and Toad book and a 95 percent accuracy rate on a 1.2 level basal selection, with acceptable comprehension of both samples. However, Betty had noted in Lakendra's assessment notebook that she was having some difficulty making sense in her writing. But it was not until both home and school acknowledged the same lingering worry that the issue came out on the table. Then Janice and Barbara were able to work together to help Lakendra's processing of ideas.

The first month of second grade Janice wrote, "She tries to read so fast when she reads to me just like a speed demon." Soon after, she reported:

Ms. Michalove, Lakendra read me the story Amelia Bedelia Goes Camping and she did a great job reading after she finished oh and by the way we stopped off at page 24. Then I asked her some questions about the story but she had to think about it before she answered. Lakendra can read the words but when it comes to asking question it looks like she has a hard time. We're going to work together every night until we get it right. Thanks. Janice B.

And work together they did. Originally there had been a focus at home on the word level of reading development. Being a good reader from Janice's point of view meant being able to read words, but as Lakendra grew more skilled at word recognition and her oral reading became more fluent, Janice shifted her focus: the process of becoming a good reader expanded to include comprehension. Barbara began to focus her interactions with Lakendra's reading on comprehension, knowing she would find support at home. Throughout second grade Janice reported to Barbara on their continued efforts to address Lakendra's understanding of what she was reading:

Janice: Ms. Michalove, Lakendra read the story of Magic Secrets (Make a pencil disappear) She can read the words real good. but it is so hard for her to tell me what she read. I really don't know what to do now. If you have any suggestions of what I can do next I am willing to listen. (12/14/92)

Barbara: Janice—Maybe try reading her stories and then discussing them together. Perhaps she is concentrating so hard on reading the words that she can't comprehend the whole story. Let me know if this helps—Thanks for being concerned and helping Lakendra. She's lucky to have a mom who cares! Ms. M.

Janice: Ms. Michalove, Lakendra brought the book home Come One Come All and she chose the Story of Curious George Get A Medal and she wanted someone to read it to her and I started and my neice wanted to finish the story. She read it and then she asked Lakendra some question about the story and Lakendra answered the question very good. Thanks. Janice B. (1/7/93)

Janice: Ms. Michalove, Lakendra read the story of Alligator Shoes and she very good with it. Lakendra concentrates on the words so hard til she can't explains what she read but I'm working with her on her sequence and I hope we will get it after awhile. Thanks. Janice B. (3/18/93)

Janice: . . . Lakendra did real well with the story we had a long detailed discussion about the story. Lakendra seems to be caughting on a little with sequence. I proud to know that she is working so hard on it. Thanks. Janice B. (4/26/93)

Mother and teachers collaborated on other decisions about the best way to help Lakendra's literacy development. By the end of first grade Lakendra had made strong progress as a reader, and Betty and Janice did not feel that she would need continued Chapter 1 reading support. Barbara agreed at the beginning of second grade. However, Janice's lingering concerns prompted them to reconsider this decision. After sharing insights about Lakendra's comprehension, they agreed she would try working with a whole language Chapter 1 teacher who could provide additional support. Janice's input had a direct impact on decision making in school on behalf of her daughter.

Growth in home and school literacy communities

Lakendra also had a say in the journal writing. As with all the children, teachers and parents adapted to meet the changing needs and abilities of the child. On April 13 in first grade Janice, trying to figure out what would be most helpful to her daughter as Lakendra developed increasing expertise, wrote:

Ms. Shockley, Lakendra has been worrying me to death about writing in her journal after she reads the story and I let her I hope it's o.k. In the story of Star the Horse she did very well and I'm glad to see her still making progress in her reading. Thanks. Janice B.

The grownups agreed that Lakendra was indeed ready to take over much of the journal writing. Lakendra commented on her opinion of books and often included dialogue of the "do you like it/yes I do" variety. She sometimes reinforced her reviews with the authoritative stance "seard [said] Lakendra." One interesting and diverse response was when she reported that she liked the story but "my mom do not." That showed us that mother and daughter discussed the stories regardless of who wrote the response, and that Lakendra understood that people can have different opinions about books.

Lakendra also was an active member of the classroom literacy community. She demonstrated her membership in several ways. She recognized that readers share books and responses within a reading community, as this April first-grade entry reveals:

> Ms. Shockley
> Good Night Moon
> was a very good
> Book This Book is Terrific
> That Renee took
> home I Bet She like
> it too.

She saw her teachers as members of the community, too, and often wrote, "You are to take this Book home too."

Lakendra's most pervasive response to literature was general evaluation:

> (11-11-91) the story Rosies walk was good
> Mrs. Shockley it was good
> Mrs. Shockley it ws good
> itwsgood
> ysitwsgood

There was growth in Lakendra's responding over time. Even in one year as a first grader, there is an obvious change from the initial series as solo writer to the end-of-year example (see Figures 5-1 and 5-2 at the end of the chapter).

By February of her second-grade year Lakendra was reading more independently and with better understanding and writing most of the responses herself. In this entry from that time we detect both pride and a continuing watchful eye as Janice wrote:

> Ms. Michalove, Lakendra read the story of Fox and his Friends and she did very good with it. She's getting better and better. As you can see I can't hardly get a chance to write in the journal for Lakendra she likes to write about her stories she read. And how is she doing in Ms. Allen's [Chapter 1 teacher's] room? Thanks. Janice Barnett

Nurturing relationships

Above all else, Lakendra's journal was about relationships. It highlighted a mother-daughter relationship of love, support, and challenge. It was also a vehicle for a teacher-to-teacher relationship building between the teaching at home and that at school. Both adults were openly appreciative of the other. Janice thanked Betty and Barbara with almost every entry and praised the efforts of her daughter. In turn, both Betty and Barbara responded with support of mother and daughter.

Lakendra became increasingly engaged with books and with writing over the course of two years. We believe one reason was that she had a way to consistently receive feedback about her literacy development from those that mattered most. Without fail, Lakendra's mother would include some kind of supportive comment about her daughter as a reader or a writer:

> As a first grader I think she's doing very good.

> Lakendra is getting along with her reading very well. In the story Mr. Grump she read right through it and I was very pleased.

> Lakendra did real good but she got a few words wrong. But altogether I think she is progressing very well.

> She did very well with this story with no problem her reading have improved a great deal and that makes me feel so good.

> In the story Fox In Love, Lakendra just wiz on through it with no problem. I think she's got reading down pack and I'm so please to see that.

This continual pride Janice showed in Lakendra's progress obviously meant a great deal to this child. Lakendra reported that her favorite thing was homework, and she made significant progress as reader and writer in the first and second grades.

Janice enjoyed telling us of the times Lakendra read to other members of her family, and she didn't hesitate to share the joy with us as Lakendra "impressed" her father and her grandfather with her reading:

> Lakendra read the story to her father and he was very pleased at the fact that she is in the 1st grade and reading books and doing so well. Thank you. Janice Barnett (9/25/91)

Lakendra's mom not only supported her daughter's work in this way but she was also quick to show her appreciation for her teachers. It was almost as if we didn't know how important such signs of success and appreciation of our efforts were to us until we had someone tell us. We remained fueled and focused by Janice's songs of praise:

> In the story Cookies Week Lakendra did very good. I really enjoy this time with her reading to me it very special for me and to me. Thanks and keep up the good work.

> Lakendra reading is improving and so is her writing. I'm glad to know Fowler Drive Teacher is so good and patient with their students. Especially you. I'm glad to know I don't have to worry about Lakendra in your class.

> I am please at the progress she has made this school year. Thanks for your good work of teaching.

> Thanks for yal great methods of teaching.

Both Betty and Barbara frequently reciprocated with supportive statements:

> Janice, Lakendra is doing well with reading and writing in class too. Thanks for taking the time to listen to her read. It really makes a difference.

> She's lucky to have such a caring mom—thanks.

> Lakendra will continue to improve with your kind of help.

> A wonderful mother.

All signs pointed to using journals as a special aspect of day-to-day literacy life. We don't know if storybook reading had been a part of the family's daily routine during Lakendra's preschool years, but we do know that it was valued and sustained on a daily basis during the first and second grades. In an early first-grade interest inventory Lakendra reported that she owned ten books. At the end of a second-grade holiday period Janice commented that they had been missing the books and were glad to be back. This led us to believe that perhaps this homework was a way to build in relationships with books a primary ingredient in their family life. We believe that the buy-in was so complete because Janice wanted to be there for her only child in an important way. She just needed an avenue of access and the respect to participate in a meaningful way.

Another example of this family's individuality was its contribution to our book *Family Stories* (1992). Instead of a narrative, they chose to list old sayings that they remembered and talked about, calling them "short stories."

Short Stories
1 When it's raining and the sun is still shining, the devil is beating his wife.
2 When it rains, God is crying and when it thunders, God is angry.
3 When a black cat crosses the road and goes to the left, it's bad luck, and to the right, it's good luck.
4 If you kill a frog you will stump your toe.
5 Open an umbrella in the house, it's bad luck.

We all—parents, children, and teachers—eventually shared a vision that reading and writing should be pleasurable, and that if forced or done in isolation, it could become a begrudged duty. Although homework was necessary, we saw that for most families it also sooner or later became desirable, a valued part of family life. And everyone wanted to keep it that way.

Janice: Ms. Michalove, Lakendra read the story of The Doorbell Rang. She did very good with it she got a little lazy tonight and didn't didn't want to write in her journal tonight she's working on some rules for her clubhouse. Well I guess that's all for now. Thanks. Janice

Barbara: It sounds like she did her writing on her clubhouse rules—good for her. I think you're great to write in the journal for her when she's involved in other writing that is important to her. Thanks. Barbara M.

It was clear that Janice saw herself as teacher. She decided that a primary purpose of the journal process was to inform—parent informing teacher, and teacher informing parent. They provided one another both general evaluation about Lakendra's reading progress and specific insights, such as singing as memorizing or "real" reading.

Despite Janice's obvious support of her daughter and her daughter's teachers, she did not show her involvement by any kind of physical presence at the school. In fact, we continue to be disturbed by the thought that in some schoolwide parent involvement programs Janice might have been discounted as a parent who did not care about the schooling of her daughter simply because she did not attend school-sponsored events. The parallel practices engaged Janice in a way that was personally meaningful, accessible, and of obvious importance to her daughter.

In her final entry at the end of first grade Janice reflected:

Ms. Shockley, Lakendra read me the story of the Hermit Crab and we both enjoyed it she wanted me to write in her journal for the last time. I really think that student journal is a great way for the parents and teachers to communicate with each other this makes me feel like I am writing or saying good-bye for the last time. I really enjoyed it. Thanks. Janice B.

Now we'd like to say again, thanks to you, Janice and Lakendra, for sharing and caring so much. We've adopted your phrase "and as always [we were] pleased."

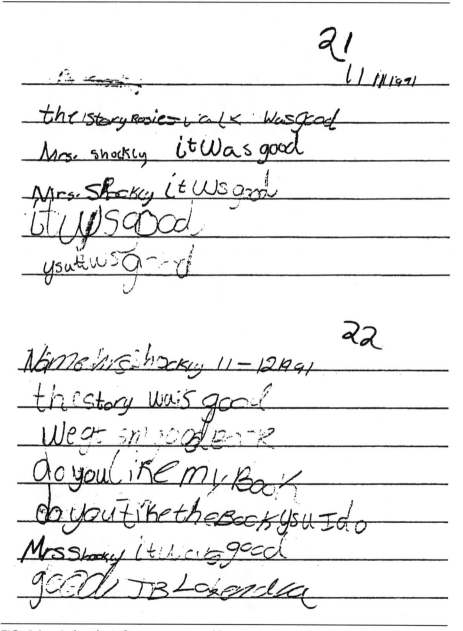

FIG. 5-1   *Lakendra's first attempts and her mother's comments*

23

11-14-1991

Mr Grump was Be good

I like the story

my mom donotkn

Mrs Shockly

tReca

11-14-91

Mrs Shockly,

As you notice for the past several days or so Lakendra has chosen to do her own response of the stories she read. I think this is good so I am going to continue to let her do so. She's spelling and sounding out a lot more words now.   Thank you

Janice Barrett

FIG. 5-1   Continued

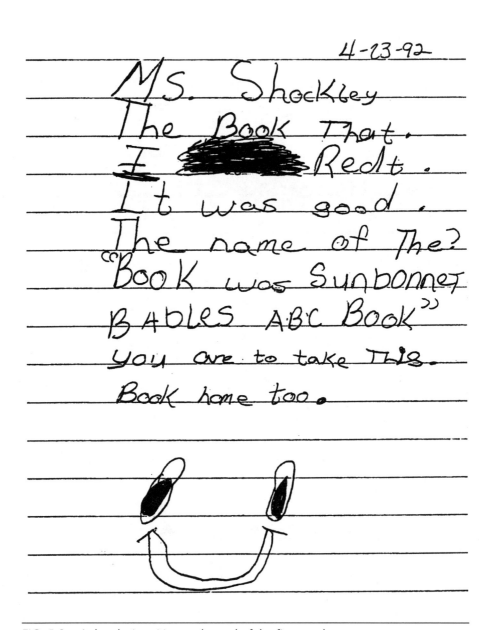

4-23-92

Ms. Shockley

The Book That.

I ~~████~~ Redt.

It was good.

The name of The?
"Book was Sunbonnet
Bables ABC Book"

you are to take This.

Book home too.

FIG. 5-2   *Lakendra's writing at the end of the first grade*

SIX
Cathy: A Book Buddy

My child is Cathy Strickland. She was born on Jan. 12, 1985 and how blessed we are to have her. We knew we had a cute, pretty, beautiful baby girl. . . . Her father Terry was so proud. Her big brother Charlie wanted a girl and I for the second time knew that motherhood was one of God's greatest blessings.

She is our early bird. She would get up in the morning and say "the sun is up, it's time to get up and I'm hungry." She likes to eat. She likes school, reading, singing, cooking, swimming, all the little girl things. And she likes dogs, tractors, sports, climbing trees and her grandparents. . . . Her grandparents have a farm. We all enjoy the farm and Cathy has two cows.

She is a Brownie Scout. . . . She has taken a lot of trips with Charlie's Cub Scout Pack because I'm a Den Leader. These are a few things I had room to tell you. How lucky we are! I hope you love her and enjoy her as much as we have. I'm always interested in my child so don't hesitate to call me if you need me for anything.

Susan Strickland

Susan's confidence in Cathy, conveyed in this initial letter, was evident in the journals also. From the beginning of first grade and continuing through second grade, Cathy was the primary person to respond in her journal. She knew she could do it, and her parents supported her efforts. It is important to note that although Cathy both read and wrote fairly independently at the beginning of first grade, her family was actively involved in her reading and writing, at various times listening to her read, discussing books, and listening to Cathy's written responses.

Reading buddies

Because Cathy wrote her own responses, she established a real dialogue about books with her teachers. At the very start of first grade, and throughout the year, Betty wrote to Cathy about the adult books she was reading. Betty's first response to Cathy, who reported that she had liked her book, was, "I'm reading a good book too. It's called *Praying for Sheetrock*. Isn't that a weird title?" This set the tone, and for two years Cathy and her teachers talked about books. They developed the kind of "grand conversations" that Eeds and Peterson (1990) suggest are the most important and natural kind of response to literature. Cathy became a real reading and writing buddy to both Betty and Barbara.

Perhaps because her teachers responded to her as a reader, Cathy developed her responses through those interactions, picking up on her partners' models. Early in first grade Betty asked a series of questions that Cathy did not answer. Betty stopped asking for several entries, then tried again. This time Cathy began answering. At first, the questions could be addressed easily with yes/no answers, and Cathy's responses were only one word, so Betty began asking more open-ended questions. For example:

January 1992
Cathy: The boy who foded [fooled] The giant. I Like This Book and I Like The giant and the boy.
Betty: What made you like them—were they smart or nice or tricky or what?
Cathy: The boy was smart. The giant was not so smart.

In April of first grade Cathy began including questions in her responses:

Cathy: *Frida's Office* I like to work because I can play and because I do not have to do it on my play day and I play all day on my play day. Wall anyway . . . I like Friday in the book and what she dase. I liked when she pute the pictures everywhere. I hope you have raid the book because it is good and I like it. How or what is your fafrant thag [favorite thing]?
Betty: I have not read that book but after your wonderful recommendation, I will! Do you want to know what my favorite book is? I have several but at the top of my list is: *Anne of Green Gables, The Education of Little Tree,* and *Ellen Foster.*

Cathy continued to ask her teachers about what they were reading and to recommend books to them through second grade. In addition, when Cathy's mother and Barbara lent books to each other, the journal became a place for them to discuss the books.

February 1993
Cathy: What are you reading, if you are reading something? Miss. C
Barbara: I am reading a book called *The Book Of Abraham.* It is about . . . I'm hoping it will get better. Right now I don't like it too much. If it doesn't get better soon, I'll probably stop reading it and read something else. Ms. M.

March 1993
Barbara: I'm glad you are enjoying so many stories in that anthology. Did you read any over the spring break? I went to the beach and read three books while I was there. One was *After Eli* by Terry Kay. I think your mom might like that one. It was about. . . . Ms. M.
Cathy: What were the other two books you read? Miss. C
Barbara: The other books I read were *The Widow's Trial* and *A Thousand Acres. The Widow's Trial* was about. . . . It was a sad book. *A Thousand Acres* was about. . . . I think your mom would like that book too. Ms. M.

May 1993
Barbara: Your mom lent me a book and I stayed up until 12:30 reading it. We may need to have naptime today! Ms. M.
Cathy and Mom: Do you like *The Firm?*
Barbara: I am still reading *The Firm.* I am enjoying it, but I feel sorry for the young lawyer and his wife. They have gotten themselves into a real mess! I hope it has a happy ending. Ms. M.

As Cathy matured as a reader, she began to share her thoughts about the books she read in a way that is similar to the way we share books with our friends. Betty noted in April, "It feels like you're talking to me on paper." Later that spring, Betty wrote, "Cathy, you are really amazing. I feel like you are my reading and writing buddy. You're always reading books that I read, and you write like me." Cathy replied, in the middle of her next response, "I know We are buddys Mrs. Shockley."

As all good book buddies do, Cathy learned to let Barbara know enough about the books she read to make them sound interesting, but she did not give away the whole plot, so that Barbara could enjoy the book for herself:

January 1993

Cathy: *Does Third Grade Last Forever?* Tracy got a stepdad . . . and hated him! I'm on chapter 3 it's a very good book. My mom wants to know, have you read this book? Miss C.

Barbara: No I haven't read that book—but I'd like to. Can I borrow it when you are finished? Maybe Tracy will like her stepdad later in the story. I hope so. It must be hard to get a stepparent that you hate! Ms. M.

Cathy: *Does Third Grade Last Forever?* Tracy gets to like her dad. I don't want to tell you all the story but I think you'll like it. Yes you can read it.

Cathy and Betty, and Cathy and Barbara, truly formed literate relationships. Cathy learned many ways of "talking about books" (Eeds and Peterson 1990) that will serve her into adulthood, as she, her mother, her teachers, and a widening literary circle share the joys of reading.

Responding to literature

Cathy showed impressive growth in her literate conversations. Her first journal response in first grade was brief: "I like it it was good my book Cathy Strickland." In comparison, her first journal response in second grade was a strong indicator of her increased abilities in responding to books:

Poems for small friends. The Book had 12 poems in it and I liked 7 of them. I liked *My travel tree* the best. I liked it the best because it reminds me of my tree that I have. (9/92)

As noted previously, Cathy often adopted models of response from her teachers. When teachers asked her questions embedded in responses, she eventfully did the same; when teachers used lots of exclamation points, so did she; when Barbara signed her entries Ms. M., Cathy signed hers Miss. C. When teachers offered more extensive kinds of responses, Cathy expanded. At one point, when Cathy had been responding simply that she liked a certain page in a book, Betty asked, "What was so good about page 2?" Cathy answered her, and in her next response (unprompted), she wrote, "I like the 5 7 pages They are both a little silly."

As Cathy interacted with books and other readers at home and at school, her literary responses became more diverse and sophisticated. By the end of first grade she had evaluated, made simple comparisons, talked about characters and events, interpreted, and identified genres she liked (including historical fiction). One of the most interesting responses was near the end of the year, when she listed not one but three reasons why she liked an Amelia Bedelia book: "1. Because it is funny. 2. I like her cactere 3. I like her. Do ya?" In February she wrote a particularly deep response: "The bears on hemlock mountain. I like this book Wane I was reding this book I beegan to thuak it was rile."

In the following sections we examine three response types that Cathy used the most: literary evaluations, characters and events, and personal connections.

Literary evaluations

Cathy almost always shared her evaluations of the books she read. When she began, she often wrote, "I like this book," or "It was good." Betty's questions prompted expanded responses. By second grade Cathy usually wrote the reasons why she thought a book was good or not so good.

October 1991
Cathy: Science is good but I can't read it. I liked looking at the pictures.
Betty: Good decision—You can learn a lot from pictures too.

October 1992
Cathy: *White Bird*. The end was sad because Nim's brother shot white bird. But you know that don't you? But I liked the book other then that. Miss. C
Barbara: Miss C. I liked *White Bird*. I thought that part was sad too. But actually I find that I like books that make me feel sad, especially when they have a happier ending. Ms. M.
Cathy: I like books like that to Miss. C.

April 1993
Cathy: *The Book of Silly Lists*. This book is about all kinds of facts. I realy did not like this book. Miss C.

Cathy's mom told us in an interest inventory sent home at the beginning of first grade that Cathy had one hundred books of her own at home. Although Cathy had not been reading long when she entered first grade, she was familiar with many books for young children. When reflecting on her reading, she often compared the book she was reading to another book she had read:

January 1992
Cathy: The True Story Of The 3 Little Pigs! I Like This Book Better Than The No't True 3 Little pigs!

February 1993
Cathy: *Perfect the Pig*. The 1st page is like Charlots web because the pigletts did not let one pig eat. Miss. Strickland
Barbara: It starts like *Charlotte's Web* but it doesn't end like it. Both authors used their imagination. Which story do you think is more believable? Ms. M.
Cathy: I think *Charlotte's Web* is more belivable. Do you? Miss. C.
Barbara: I agree. I think *Charlotte's Web* is more believable than *Perfect the Pig*. I *know* a pig could never fly—but I'm not absolutely sure that animals don't talk to each other. Love, Ms. M.

Cathy's literary criteria had obviously grown, from the standard "I like it because it is good/It's good because I like it" to emotive elements, book comparisons, and expressions of preference for fiction over nonfiction and for more realistic over less realistic fiction.

Characters and events

Cathy also wrote about characters and events in the books she read. We asked questions that encouraged her to build on her responses. Discussing the books we read was an integral part of our classroom routines, and Cathy was used to talking about characters, settings, and events. Students shared books with other students and acted out stories they had read. Cathy had been exposed formally and informally to a variety of ways to respond to books. As she began to read longer chapter books, the questions were real questions between two readers who were not reading the same book:

October 1992
Cathy: The Boxcar children I like when Henry said "Land Ho!" Miss. C.
Barbara: Are they in a boat? it sounds like it—or up in a hot air balloon. What mystery are the Boxcar Children trying to solve in this book? Ms. M.
Cathy: Boxcar Children Blue Bag Mystery #6 The Boxcar Children were traveling in a boat to an island. This mystery is about what happens to them on this deserted island. In chapter six they found a big statue which had fallen to the ground. But I think there is some one else on the island. Cathy and Mom
Barbara: Aha . . . you are beginning to think like a detective! I wonder why there would be a big statue on an island where there are no people. What happened next? Ms. M.
Cathy: Whll . . . they find a turtle shall that has a pattern that they think someone elce karved the pattern on the turtle shall. they sow the tree move when the wind was not bloing and a coknut fell. I thit that was ale.
Barbara: It certainly sounds like someone else is on that island. . . . I hope whoever it is—is nice to them.
Cathy: The Boxcar children Someome is on the island and it is Peter. they fond him and are living together. the next chper is Eight in the Family and that makes me thik that peter has joned the Family. Because they said That Peter could jone the Family if they could not fined his Family. Miss. C.
Barbara: Miss C. You certainly sound like a good detective! Maybe you will be a detective when you grow up. Ms. M.
Cathy: *The Boxcar Children* I'm not sach a detective but I might be one. I can not beleve I have read so many Boxcar Children books. But I'm loving them.

Cathy read fourteen books from the Boxcar Children series while she was in second grade. She had begun her fascination with mysteries in first grade; Betty shared with Cathy her own favorite mystery writer, Mary Higgins Clark. Mysteries, like realistic fiction, seemed to provide Cathy a way to enter the story world. She was right there with the main character, trying to solve the puzzle. After reading *Nate the Great and the Halloween Hunt* in February of first grade, Cathy wrote:

> I wanld love to be a datltaf [detective] wald you? I rilly like this Book. I thack I no the anger [answer] to the 22 paeg and I thack it is the cats hoppling out. Maeking the

CLINKING and the CLANKING and the SHRIEKING or sume chker or trter's [tricker or treaters]. do you thaek you no who was maeking the nowees?

She continued to enjoy mysteries in second grade, writing in November, "I finished the book and will soon be reading another mystery."

Cathy identified other genres that she liked as she became an independent reader during the latter half of first grade. In April of that year she wrote about the book Betty was reading to the class, which she was reading on her own:

> The Little House In the big Woods I Like This Book Because it is historical Fiction It Reminds me of The Little house on the Prairie and I Like the Little House on The prairie. I'm on page 146 The class has a lot of pages to go.

Personal connections

Cathy made personal connections to most of the books she chose to read. It was clear that reading was important to her. She often shared thoughts that arose from her readings. At the end of second grade her mom told us in a parent response survey that "Cathy has really developed a love for reading. She has become a very strong and independent reader." As the following two entries show, Cathy made personal connections early in first grade, and Betty reinforced this new development. Over time, the responses became more extensive and specific as Cathy's literacy developed.

October 1991
Cathy: Boo Bear and the Kite I like to fly a Kite in My Back yard.
Betty: This is a very nice response Cathy. You have thought about the book and how it is connected to your own life.

October 1992
Cathy: *The Boxcar Children* I liked the chapter Fire! Because, well I jist liked it. I have reprted 2 fires at the same house. When I go by a fire I'm skared that it will spred.

At the beginning of second grade, when Barbara asked parents to "tell me about your child," Cathy's mom wrote, "She loves life, smiles a lot and loves her family." Cathy's family was central in her responses to literature. She frequently related a story to her own life and family experiences. The stories her family contributed to the *Family Stories* class books also reflected this strong sense of family. In first grade the families worked together and contributed one story to the class book. In second grade the children each wrote a story at school, then asked their parents to contribute a story from their own lives.

A Very Special Person
By Cathy Strickland's family

I got a trophy from my granddaddy before he died. He told me to take care of it for him. It was sad when he died. We did a lot of things together before he got sick. We read books, told stories, sang songs like "Did You Ever Go A Fishin' on a Pretty Bright Day?," "She'll be Comin' Around the Mountain," "Oh, the Beef Steak, It Was Rare."

We went to the Sale Barn and looked at cows, horses, pigs, and goats. I had fun with my granddaddy. We would check the cows, ride in the pick-up truck, walk in the pasture. We would go down to the fish pond and fish. I caught a lot of fish and so did he. We would swing in the hammock, have a picnic on the tailgate of the truck, and eat vienna sausage—yum, yum.

      He gave me Star, my horse. She is pretty and I love to ride her. My granddaddy was a very special person.

The journal became a place for Cathy to express some of her feelings at a difficult time in her life. After her grandfather died during her year in first grade, she made many personal connections with Betty and the books she was reading:

February 1992

Cathy: Can you hear Me Grandad? I like this Book. and it reminds me of me and my Grandad. My Grandad always listened to me. He had a big Chair That he set in. He would read me Books. and we would have a Good Time toghether. We would Go fishing. and this reminds Me of famleis.

Betty: Cathy, this is such a special response. I hope you always remember those good times with your grandfather. My grandfather died when I was 5, but I still remember the corn candy he used to have for me and playing hide and go seek.

February 1992

Cathy: The bears on hemlock Mountain. . . . it was Exciting. it was a good Book. as fare as i got to. it was good. I will take the Book home tomorrow. and finish reading it. I like to read Books thit are Excitinng. do you like to? Me and my Grinndad youste to read Books theyt were good. wane i read a Book it ramies me of my Griandad.

Betty: I like to read books that are exciting too. . . . I think your grandfather would be very happy knowing he helped make reading a wonderful time for you.

For Cathy, books were a way of connecting with people, including family members and teachers. They also proved to be a way of staying connected with memories of her grandfather. As we see in the next section, the tradition of telling family stories was a rich one for the Stricklands.

Family stories

Cathy had many books in her home, and reading was a family activity. When Cathy's parents contributed to our classroom collections of family stories, she was able to see her parents as writers too. We can guess that these stories have been told orally many times, just as in the classroom, where children had opportunities to talk through their ideas before committing them to print.

      Sharing family stories stretched the classroom community to include a wider group of people. All of us caught a glimpse of one another's family members and often a glimpse of the past. Family lore became classroom community lore through the writing of the stories. The family stories helped this diverse group of learners see the similarities among themselves.

      Everyone's story was valued equally. The stories were published in classroom books and read again and again by the students. The children felt a real sense of pride as their parents' stories were displayed alongside favorite classroom authors. Family stories put the spotlight on the children as they brought them into school to share with their classmates. Cathy shone with pride as her teacher read the stories that her mom and dad contributed to the class collection:

Granny's Backyard
By Susan Strickland (Mom)

I wish you could have seen my Granny's backyard. It was beautiful. There were many tall pine trees, big pecan trees, azalea bushes, dogwoods and day lillies. A perfect place to play hide and seek, have your own hide out and make up wild west stories.

Back then we always traveled by horseback. I'm talking about stick horses. They were made from bamboo poles or left over lumber found around the house. We tied a string around the top of the stick and it was the reins, Granny's garage was the stable. They were all lined up. Trigger, Black Beauty, Silver, Lady and several more. All of the neighborhood children had their own horse. We would spend hours running our little legs off on those stick horses.

My brother Chuck and my cousin Peggy and I would play Roy Rogers and Dale Evans. Roy Rogers, king of the cowboys, would be busy taking care of the bank robbers—putting them in jail. Dale Evans would meet him down the path and they would sing "Happy Trails to You" and ride off into the sunset.

We could change the story anytime we would like. The ranch was under a big sweet gum tree. Town was on the other side of the big yard. Sometimes we would have Roy married to a younger lady named Judy Rogers. What fun we had!

Princess
By Terry Strickland (Dad)

I remember the weekend we visited my Uncle Jeff in Griffin, Georgia. He raised Holstein dairy cows on his farm. A new calf was born that very day and he gave it to me as a gift. We (Dad, Mom, Aunt Eula and me) traveled home with Princess in the backseat of our 1956 Montclair Mercury. She was wrapped in a burlap bag diaper.

It took a lot of time to feed her four times a day with a bottle, but I did it and she grew up to be a big Holstein cow. Everytime Princess had a calf of her own we would buy a calf to put with her, because she gave so much milk. Her mother gave 13-15 gallons of milk a day for the dairy.

One summer day I went down to check on Princess. She had had a baby calf near the fish pond. I picked it up and took it back to the barn, then went down to get Princess. When I got back to Princess that baby calf had beat me back. How could this happen? So I picked up the calf again and went back to the barn. When I got to the barn, there was the first calf. Twins! She had twins! I went back down to get Princess and there was another calf. Triplets, she had had triplets! She gave plenty of milk and raised them all.

Those three calves grew up and had calves of their own. Mom and Dad saved the money made from my calves and it helped put me through college.

These stories, like so many that family members contributed both years, not only introduced us to an extended family of moms, dads, aunts, uncles, cousins, and grandparents but also served as historical treasures wrapped in narrative. From Susan and Terry's contributions, we as a class learned about children's games (riding stick horses and playing cowboys), folk heroes Roy Rogers and Dale Evans, and raising calves.

A valuable lesson in partnership

The journals provided a place for Cathy to grow as a writer and provided a stimulus to think about and discuss the books she read. They also gave parents a vehicle to communicate with their child's teacher. Cathy's mom wrote this letter to Barbara at the end of second grade. It gave us a glimpse into the importance of the response journals for the children's parents and the sense of community that had spread from the school-room to include families in their child's education.

> In these two years of our classroom project I have seen how communication has made a difference. You have done a great job of meeting the needs of each child and each family. Something every teacher has to do but I feel it has been easier with this line of communication at least from the parent stand point. . . . We have learned a valuable lesson—to keep the lines of communication open and I'm sure this group will communicate. . . . Keep in touch over the summer and let me know if you read any good books. Thanks a million. Susan Strickland

Susan learned through the invitations how important communication was, and learned some very enjoyable ways of sharing home and school information, but we learned something just as valuable. Two people who looked at Cathy's journals remarked on how "uninvolved" the parents were. How wrong they were, and how important it is for all of us not to judge by appearances.

From her letter it is clear that Susan *was* very involved even though she rarely wrote in the journal. She discussed Cathy's reading with her, read over her journal entries, and scaffolded Cathy's step into longer chapter books. Cathy's mom saw the journal as a line of communication to the teacher even though she rarely used it in the direct ways we saw in Adrian's and Lakendra's families. The journal gave Cathy's mom a look into what Cathy was doing in school. We found that when they were given the opportunity for genuine dialogue and a sense of belonging, parents formed real partnerships with their child's teacher. They formed them according to their family style and needs, and each relationship was different, because each family is different.

LITERACY
CONNECTIONS

SEVEN

Family-Teacher Connections

F amilies have their own "funds of knowledge," according to a group of school-based and university-based teachers and researchers in Tucson (Moll et al., 1992). While some teachers may talk about children as coming to school "with no background" or "no home experiences" (see interviews by Fraatz, 1987), Moll et al. point out that every child has a background of learning experiences and usually a network of people who support various kinds of learning. These networks are often "flexible, adaptive, and active, and may involve multiple persons from outside the homes" (p. 133). Indeed, many of the relationships we formed with families involved several people, both within and outside the home.

Moll et al. explain that within these networks members establish " 'confianza' (mutual trust), which is reestablished or confirmed with each exchange, and leads to the development of long-term relationships . . . [and] constantly provides contexts in which learning can occur" (p. 134). The parallel practices, especially the journals, seemed to provide that dependable context for learning and to be the vehicle for establishing mutual trust. Moll and colleagues note that "teachers rarely draw on the resources of the 'funds of knowledge' of the child's world outside the context of the classroom" (p. 134). However, through our communication with families, we were able to draw on these funds, to develop long-term relationships, and to learn from (and share information with) family members concerning each child as a literacy learner and a human being.

The key seemed to be in recognizing what was positive in each family's journal, then making those perceptions known to the family. Each teacher journal entry was a genuine response to what the parent or child had written the previous night. Here are a few examples from our classrooms:

• When LaToya's mom wrote about the book being so long that they decided to put it down and read some more later, Betty responded, "Perfect! That's what I would have done too."

In this section we explore the connections among readers and texts. The connections in this and the next three chapters are presented from four perspectives as two-way connections, although most times there was a four-way connection: book-child-family-teacher. This some-what artificial separation serves as an organizing convenience. Some of the excerpts may illuminate another kind of connection as well: for example, a teacher-child connection may also provide insight into a reader-book connection. As a reader, you have the right, even the responsibility, to "move" chunks of data to fit your own understanding of how the parallel literacy practices affected teachers, children, and families.

- Another time, LaToya's mom wrote about the fun they had reading. Betty responded, "I'm going to recommend your house for story time for all little children."
- Renee's parents wrote about their concerns over Renee's choice of books. Betty gave them some information to help them understand Renee's reading development and added, "Thanks for sharing your thoughts and concerns with me."
- Brandon's mom wrote about the frustrations Brandon was experiencing with his reading. She included what she had done to relieve his frustrations. Barbara responded, "Good work, Mom! . . . Brandon's so lucky to have you to help him."

Families voiced great appreciation for the journals as an avenue of communication with Betty and Barbara. Several said they liked knowing they didn't have to wait until parent-teacher conferences to discuss issues, be they large (Does my child need a tutor?) or small (What happened on the playground yesterday?). Other families reported that they were always interested to see what the teacher wrote in response to the family's entry. Still others regularly relied on this channel to provide and solicit information about their child's literacy progress. Families said they valued having the journal available to communicate with the teacher. In a discussion at the end-of-year parent meeting, one mother explained:

> I think it's wonderful to have that resource whether you use it or not. . . . Like, there hasn't been a lot that we've written back and forth, but I've occasionally put something in there with an asterisk to ask you about it. I think it's wonderful to be able to have that kind of communication. . . . I know it's a source that you're going to see as opposed to me trying to catch you on the phone. I mean, you're as much a mommy as I am at night. And I don't . . . want to have to call you then. During the day you have to either rely on a message getting through and it's, you know, not fair to interrupt your day there . . . and you know some of these [issues] that could be addressed very quickly can go on, you know, a day or so, and when you're anxious about something . . . I could just put a note in the journal and say, you know, "We really need to talk today about something that's going on," and I feel like my concerns are going to be addressed or if you had a concern about something it's going to be addressed. I think it's great.

Sharing information about literacy development

When we made suggestions, just as we would with any other colleague, we let families know we respected their opinions. We used phrases such as "I wonder how it would work if . . . ," "You might try . . . ," and "I noticed that [your child] is having trouble with . . . One way you could help is . . . ." Families seemed to be very receptive to information offered in a nonthreatening manner.

LaToya's mother worried about her daughter's progress. She used the journal to talk over her concerns with Betty and Barbara, and to get advice. At the beginning of first grade Mom had the impression that LaToya was behind, that she needed a tutor. Even though LaToya made marked progress that year, and her mom noted her progress at times, at other times she continued to worry—right up to the end-of-first-grade evaluation. In June she wrote, "She's reading pretty good, but not where she should be at this age." By the end of second grade, however, LaToya's mother saw her child as a competent reader: "LaToya has really surprised me with the way she is reading. I thought for a while she would never get the hang of reading but now she can read almost anything she wants and that really makes me feel good." This really emphasized to us the importance of more than one year of both whole language instruction and home-school connections.

In LaToya's case, as with several families, the regular correspondence served a reciprocal purpose. The families informed the teacher about their child, providing valuable information about how the child was interacting with them during these literacy events. Families wrote about who the child read with, what strategies they used in reading the book, what the child thought about the book, and any difficulties or triumphs the child might have had reading or writing about the book. In return, the teachers informed families about how their child was developing in the context of classroom interactions. In addition, Betty and Barbara wrote about children as readers and writers in general, so families could see their child in a broader perspective of literacy development. That may have been reassuring, to get feedback and information from someone who knows a lot about children this age and who could tell them where their child fit in.

Brandon's mom and Betty acted as partners in helping Brandon and helping each other. Both of them worried about him at the beginning of the year and shared information about how he was doing. Kathryn informed Betty about what he learned, what she worked on with him, his spelling, his preference for stories, word analysis insights, reading processes, his lack of concentration on a long book, his past school problems, his frustrations, a new stage in his reading development, and his pride in his school work when he really started making progress. She scaffolded Brandon's learning all year and talked with Betty teacher-to-teacher about her decisions and concerns. An example of the sharing between these two teachers (and mothers) took place in early January, after Brandon and his mother had read *Heckedy Peg:*

Kathryn: [book response] . . . I asked him to recite the days of the week starting with Sunday. He did but left out Saturday. When I asked him to try again, he got very upset and started to cry. I just didn't understand the reason why and he wouldn't tell me.

Betty: Brandon reminds me of my son Jamie when he was that age (He's a junior in high school now!) Jamie knew I had high expectations for him and he didn't want to disappoint me. Every time I put him on the line so he had to make his "faults" visible or obvious, he would crumble. I'd suggest making a point to let Brandon enjoy being close to you with a book to share—then letting him choose something he knows he does well to share with you, then maybe point out one new thing you'd like to teach him or have him learn from the experience. Does this make any sense?

Kathryn: This makes a lot of sense. I guess I have forgotten that Brandon was like this. When he was younger, learning new things like tying his shoes, he would get very upset with himself and cry and cry until he accomplished what he wanted to learn. Thank you for sharing that with me.

The next year, at the March parent-teacher conference, Kathryn shared with Barbara her concern that Brandon's father was putting too much pressure on him to sound out every word during times they read together at home. Barbara wrote the next day in the journal:

> To Dad—George—when Brandon read to me the other day I noticed that he has a hard time when he comes to a word he doesn't know. One way to help him with that is to ask him to skip it and read to the end of the sentence. Then go back and think "what makes sense here." Encourage him to take a guess then check the letters to see if perhaps it is correct. I feel like developing this strategy will help him because so often in English a word is not spelled how one might imagine. Thanks—Barbara Michalove

Apparently, this suggestion for an alternative strategy was well received. Kathryn wrote back, "Your message to George really worked—thank you."

Rick's mother, Cathy, also formed a close working relationship with Betty through the home-school journal. She wrote almost every night, many times sharing how she was teaching Rick and asking Betty for advice (or offering her some):

Cathy: I Reed the Book about used cars and after I got threw I asked Rick what it was about and he explained it to me. (10/15)

Betty: Reading to Rick and having him explain it to you sounds like a good deal. I hope you both enjoyed your time together.

Soon after this entry, Betty wrote a note to Rick in the journal, encouraging him to write sometimes. Cathy responded the next day, "Rick was going to write you a Note But he forgot to he did read his Book." The next night she wrote:

Cathy: Rick and me Read 3 Little Book, I can't get him to write in this Note Book for us I think for Christmas I will get him so[me] Books with the tape so he can Listen and Lern more. (11/13)

Betty: That's a great idea. He likes to use our listening center. It's OK if he doesn't write in this journal yet. I bet he will feel comfortable doing [it] a little later in the year.

Cathy: Can you think of anything I can get Rick for Christmas that might help him in School for Learning if so Let me know befor xmas okay (11/17)

Betty: I think you had the best idea yesterday with the books and tapes. I always think a nice gift is paper and pencils and markers too.

In December, Cathy made another instructional decision about her child, and Betty responded with both respect and advice:

Cathy: I Read the Book to Rick would you try to get him to take some Christmas Books too We have stoped the (ABC) now I'm going to let him write differet words and learn to spell I think that will be a big help for him what do you think.

Betty: I think most anything you choose to do with Rick will be helpful because I know how well you work together. I would suggest however that you make sure the actual reading time is always pleasant and interesting for Rick. If we try to test him by saying things like—now spell the words in your story—we could cause alot of worry. I'll suggest some Christmas books. Thanks again for all you do.

Cathy: Your idea is much better thanks Alot I will keep Reading to Rick Because I really enjoy it myself.

In February, Cathy had another idea about how to help her child:

Cathy: I'm thinking about Letting Rick take easy words that he knows and make storys out of them what do you think
Betty: I'd say give it a try. Let me know how it goes—O.K.?

The connection between Betty and this family extended to the father, too. Betty had learned that he was an excellent artist and mechanic, and he worked on her car that year. One day he wrote in the journal, "Miss Shockley You are one of the greates Teachers I have ever know and one of nised"

All Rick's teachers, at home and at school, began to see progress. Rick began the year referred for special services for both behavior and learning needs. As a writer, Rick moved from frequently unfinished illustrations without print to writing independently, using a mix of conventional and invented spelling. As a reader, he moved from picture-governed and personal oral storytelling not connected to books to print-governed emergent reading that made use of all the cuing systems. Betty and Cathy were encouraged:

Cathy: He's learning more every Day I'm proud. (3/5) Rick Read some of his Book By hisself. He's Learning so much. (3/11)
Betty: He really is! I hope this is the beginning of a real life interest in reading and writing for him. Alot of his success is certainly because of your time and love. Congratulations to you both!

Rick was making so much progress that Betty again brought up the idea of Rick's writing:

Betty: I think it's time for Rick to write about his books now—I'll look forward to reading what you write Rick.
Rick: PeTeR Rabbit IT WAS ABOUT MR. MCGReGOR and PeTeR WHO WAS NAUGHTY and dId'nt DO WhAT his MOTHeR SAId The End

Rick was promoted to second grade. In another kind of classroom, without these home-school connections and the constant support and interaction they offered, Rick would most likely have repeated first grade. We still worry about him. But we also have great hope that a child who made this much progress, a child who has parents that work so hard at helping him be successful, will become a lifelong reader and writer.

Hearing children's voices

The parallel practices of "tell me about your child," home-school journals, and parent-child-teacher reflection provided another, more subtle benefit. We noticed it with Renee, and Kimberly's mother spelled it out for us.

Through the multiple communication channels Betty established, she had the opportunity to know how much the family cared about and supported Renee, and to keep this shy child, who might have faded into the background, in her mind every day. Renee, more than any other child, established her place in the classroom community first through the voice of her family. Renee took over the journal writing in second grade after an opening message from her mom. She read with her sister and her mother, but she wrote all the responses herself. If we had not known how involved Renee's family was in her literacy from the year before, we might have missed that these continued to be family literacy events and might have pictured an isolated reader and writer. Instead, the two-way communication channels ensured that both Renee and her family would be heard.

Kimberly's mother saw the journal as a way for children's voices to be honored (Oldfather, 1993), for children to be really heard. She also saw an open channel of communication between teacher and parent, and she used it to share her joy and insights about her daughter with her teachers. She wrote, after a parent meeting early in second grade:

> I think this is a wonderful thing you are doing. Having children and parents interacting with each other. Giving their own ideas about things. I think thats important to express their own ideas and be able to have someone to listen to those ideas. Kimberly is a one in a million child, shes lovable, she has her own ideas about things and a very lovable personality, she knows when you are not listening to her and she will tell you.

Having two venues for reading probably helped all the children become more confident about their reading, because they read more often and to a variety of audiences. However, the home-school practices may have been particularly beneficial to two students who did not want to take risks in one setting or the other. Brad practiced new books with his mom first, before he took risks in the classroom community. Brad had experienced rejection and failure in his previous school and did not come into first grade willing to risk new behaviors. Chris, on the other hand, frequently read books several times at school before he took them home to read with his parents, who had very high expectations for his reading. These voices, which might literally have been stilled if Chris and Brad had had only one place where people listened to them read, grew in confidence in both settings.

Cultivating personal relationships

Betty made a direct attempt to establish a positive relationship between Brad, his mom, and the school. They had not had this relationship at Brad's previous school. The journal served this purpose. Betty built Brad up, as did his mother; they both talked with pride about Brad's progress. At the beginning of second grade, in response to Barbara's invitation to "tell me about your child," his mom wrote:

> Brad is a child who tries hard to be liked and make friends. He is sometimes unsure of himself at school because of a bad experience at [another school]. He had a great, fantastic wonderful school year last year and I hope this year is successful as last year.

Each relationship was special. In some cases, Betty and Barbara already knew the families, from teaching an older child or from community connections. One such relationship was with Sara, Colin's mom. Betty had taught Colin's older sister Erin three years earlier. Betty and Sara also connected as readers; Sara mentioned her own reading in the journal. At the end of the year, in writing what a wonderful experience the journal had been, she wrote, "Perhaps if I kept a journal of the books I read, I wouldn't forget them so quickly." Betty talked more about herself as a reader in this journal. She recommended books, talked about books she liked and disliked, and shared "insider information" about authors: she had met Graeme Base, and she shared that James Marshall was both author and illustrator. Betty and Sara truly had "grand conversations" (Eeds and Peterson, 1990) about books.

Each family used the journal in a different, highly personal way to connect with their child's teacher. Like the home visits that teachers in the Moll et al. (1992) study made, we think the regular journal dialoguing helped "establish a new, more symmetrical relationship with the parents of the students" (p. 139). The focus was on the child's emergent literacy and interaction during literacy events. This kind of home-school dialogue may be a key element for school success, especially for children teachers worry about.

In a study of first-grade children whose kindergarten teachers had predicted they would be unsuccessful, Goldenberg (1989) found that specific communication between parents and teachers, focused on learning to read and what parents could do to help their children, made the difference for children who were successful in first grade, contrary to predictions. He stated, "Neither language-minority, low-economic, nor low-education status were obstacles to parents' ability or willingness to help their children learn to read" (p. 63). However, "parent contact in and of itself is not sufficient. The *substance* of the content must be such that it prompts parents to act in ways that will help the child academically" (p. 64).

We agree. The journals and other transactions between families and teachers were literacy-oriented. Betty and Barbara did not report on how children behaved in class, handled other school tasks, or got along with each other. The journals were not "what I did in school" or "what I did at home" diaries, but literature response journals that were open-ended, allowing for communication that was important to the participants. Teachers and families talked in the journals in ways that are usually impossible because of time, distance, and tradition. We learned that when the adults who care most about children have this ongoing, open forum, they learn from each other and can work in concert to support children as growing, engaged readers and writers.

EIGHT
Family-Child Connections

> Family storybook reading is a time when parents and children create their own special kind of magic. Whatever happens during the day, sharing storybooks brings the family together. Just a few minutes into a book and busy schedules are left behind, accidents are forgotten, and bad tempers fade. (Taylor and Strickland, 1986, p. 3)

The reading, talking, and journal writing process gave every family a dependable time to spend together around books. Several parents commented that the structure helped them do something they wanted to do, read with their children, at times when the routines of everyday life might otherwise have intruded. Families found ways to connect with their children even when they were not directly represented (i.e., no adult writing) in the journals: some listened to the child read, some discussed the book with the child, some read or listened to the child's written responses. Some children interacted with one family member throughout; others read and wrote with mothers, fathers, grandparents, aunts, brothers, sisters, cousins, and family friends.

Family literacy networks

Books were a way for Renee to connect with many people at home. Most often she read with her mother's friend, who signed each thoughtful entry "J. Miller." Renee reported that they read to each other and that sometimes he read "and I repeated after him." She also read to her mom, brother, and sister. As Betty wrote to Renee, "You seem to be making a lot of people happy with your reading."

Renee was a child Betty had worried about at the beginning of the year; she seemed withdrawn and reluctant to take risks. However, she progressed as a reader from not attempting the informal reading inventory passage in August to reading a first-grade passage with 91 percent accuracy at the end of the year. Betty attributed this progress to reading so much with family (at home) and friends (at school). As noted earlier, Renee's mother believed "60% of her learning was from her teacher, 40% was from at home with her parents."

What was it about this family literacy event that made it so important? Ralph Fletcher (1993), noted educational consultant, suggests, "It's not just the book you share, it's the relationship you have with the book that comes through to the child." Adam's mom recognized this truth when she pinpointed the power of parent-child-book interactions:

Adam started bringing books home from school If *I* was excited about the book. And let him know I was and realy wanted to hear him read. He would be very much so. I would always tell him, Adam be sure and get Us another book to read. . . . In short, If I was excited and wanted to hear his books, So Was He.

Adam concurred. When he reflected at the end of first grade on how he had learned to read, he wrote, "My mom tolt me read. I can read good. My mom tot me how to read from the books at scool." Near the end of first grade, Betty listened to Adam read a book from the classroom library and asked him how he had learned to read so well. He replied, "My mom taught me. When you let us take the books home every night, my mom read them to me and then I started reading to her!"

Adam did not report having any books of his own, so this nightly access to school books provided mother and son an opportunity they might not otherwise have had. Some definitions of a person who is highly literate might include standards of conventional writing; on the contrary, we would argue that parents who read and enjoy literature are more literate than many adults who may be good spellers or capable readers but who don't read. Adam's mom designed a way to support her own literacy in the journal responses: "Sometimes I write and Adam reads and spell's lot's of word's for me from the book." This may have contributed to Adam's growing understanding of *word* and to his spelling; it certainly showed him that even adults have different approaches to reading and writing.

Adam's father and older brother also created unique ways of recording his responses, his father by page number ("On page 23 I like the Rhamphorynchus has a long tail") and his brother, Richard, by recording a list of likes and dislikes ("Adam likes the nice girl," "Adam dont like the mean girls"). Richard carried his role as big brother over to the journal. After the "likes/dislikes" entry he wrote

notes:
and = &, or, [variation of ampersand]
[both variations drawn again, this time with arrows indicating how to draw them]
I is allways capitalize unless it is in a word, *also!* allways capitalize the first letter in a sentence. Also you capitaise! *pronouns:* such as people's names, places that are specific, cities, states, captals, country

Richard and Adam may or may not talk about books, but there is a literacy connection between them. Richard was going to make sure that his little brother had explicit information about rules of conventional English.

Younger siblings were often direct beneficiaries of home reading events. Dumoneak's sister, whom she read to all the time, was Elmira. Elmira's kindergarten teacher mentioned to Barbara what a good reader Elmira was. Like Elmira, Brad's little brother, Wesley, was the beneficiary of story time. In second grade Brad's mother wrote, "Brad read the whole book to Wesley and I. We really enjoyed his reading. . . . I'm proud of him being able to read me a story so well." Barbara wrote to Brad, "Wesley is lucky to have a big brother like you to read him stories." We are not only preparing readers of today, but parents of tomorrow. Children have a model of parental literacy during school years, and they are already engaging in reading to younger siblings. Durkin (1966) found in her study of children who read early that many of them had older siblings who read to them.

A forum for family values

LaToya and her family really talked about books. Her mom, and sometimes dad, often extended the story with LaToya, as when they "made up some jokes and had fun" after *Spooky Riddles,* made up stories about the pictures in *The Big Hungry Bear,* and even fixed "chicken soup with rice" for dinner after reading Sendak's book. They made personal connections, drawing on their family life, such as talking about ways LaToya "cut up" like the characters in her book, how she was "always wishing for thing she don't need" like the character in *A Wish for Wings that Work,* and her insight after reading *Max's Christmas:* "You can't fool me I know who Santa is moma, and thank you for buying my toys."

This family went beyond everyday personal connections to deeper family connections in their conversations. In October of second grade her mother wrote:

> LaToya read "Follow the Drinking Gourd." I enjoyed this book with LaToya. I am glad she is finding books to read about her own people. She asked me alot of questions about slaves and white people and why they hate each other. and why she should be proud to be black. She had so many questions it took us 1½ hours to read this book and for me to explain things to her. Mary

Barbara told Mary that she and LaToya would look in the school library for more books about her heritage, and they did. LaToya and her mom read one together the next night and wrote:

> We read the book "Runaway Slave." It was a good book. We took turns reading pages. The book was kinda long but everytime we put it down we want to pick it back up to find out the ending.

Many researchers are interested in defining engagement. We think Mary has it: "Everytime we put [the book] down we want to pick it back up." For LaToya and her mother, the engagement was not just with the pleasure of reading, but with significant ideas. Books became an information source, and a forum for important family discussions of cultural pride and history.

The relationships families formed around books gave many of the children a strong sense of how much their parents valued literacy and what a commitment they made to helping their children do well in school. LaToya's mother reported in September of second grade:

> LaToya read this book to me and father. She enjoyed reading this book. Time she got home she wanted to read, but I told her to wait for awhile and she said, "Mama you know reading my book is just as important as anything else so let's read my book." So we had to sit down and read that book first thing. She did a pretty good job.

In March, Mary again reported with pride on LaToya's sense of how important reading was in their lives: "She told me 'Mom come on cut the T.V. off because reading is more important than T.V.' She seems to be excited with reading now. She tries to do alot of reading on her own." Mary had been worried about her daughter's reading development earlier in the year; now she could see LaToya's progress and her own role in that exciting development. She had good insights about LaToya's progress. In May she wrote, "She had read this book before, but it was interesting to listen to her read and think about how she use to read."

Support of literacy did not take the same form in every family. For example, Bryan and his mother Denese created a unique partnership through the journal. For the first few months in first grade Denese drew an illustration to go along with the book. Often, Bryan colored the picture, picking up on what his mother had identified at the beginning of the year as his main interest: coloring. Betty applauded these responses and connected them with published author-illustrators:

> Your mom is a good illustrator and you are a good colorer. You know that's what Audrey and Don Wood did sometimes. Don would color in what Audrey drew.

In November, Betty asked Bryan to write at least a sentence, but she did not want to lose the tie between mother and son. When she wrote to Denese explaining the request, she said, "He still wants to read his book with you and for you to do an illustration but then he will write about the story and/or the illustrations." This pattern continued in second grade, with either Bryan or his mom illustrating nearly every story. Other dynamics changed—Bryan read more independently, Denese read chapter books to him, Denese wrote longer, dictated responses—but the real connection between mother and son was art. The journal provided a forum for this talent, and an appreciative audience.

It was not always obvious that parents were involved with their children's nightly reading. A cursory look at Dumoneak's journals does not reveal the extent of her family support. Dumoneak wrote nearly every entry herself. However, Dumoneak's reading and writing were a family affair. Her whole family was involved at various times in the first and second grades, including cousins and friends who happened to be visiting during reading time. In first grade she wrote, "We all injoy it and my brother injoy it my sisters injoy it and my dad injoy it and my mama injoy it to and I injoy it." This involvement continued in second grade:

> The book that I read was good it was call Martin's Mice. I like it. i read it to my sister for a bedtime story she said when she was on the bus she said it was really, really, really,, really, good and I said it was good two it was really. good, good, good, good. My Mother siad it was good My brother siad it was super good. my sister said it was really good. (4/4)

Kimberly was also an independent journal writer. As she announced proudly, "I write by myself—my mom don't help me." It was not until a parent meeting, when we were seeking family insights on two years of journal communication, that we learned from Kimberly's mother that although they did not write together in the journal, writing had a very real role in their relationship. She and JoBeth shared stories, mother to mother, about family writing:

JoBeth: I just was thinking when you were talking that when we were getting ready to move here from Kansas, my daughter was about 14 and it was a real, real hard time. She didn't want to move. She was real, real angry with me. I mean, all kinds of stuff. We just couldn't even talk to each other at all. And so we started a dialogue journal, kind of like these.

K: Kimberly and I write notes back to each other all the time.

JoBeth: And it let us cool down in between, you know, sometimes it was a couple of days before we cooled down enough to talk back to each other. But it really got us through a hard time.

K: Yeah, we do, we run a piece of paper where we write things back and forth so that nobody gets angry. She writes all sorts of stuff to me and then I write things back to her and eventually it, you know, it works its way down and then it's interesting to go back and look at the progression of the, you know, of the discussion/argument about something. But it's a way to be able to, you know, to have a dialogue, and I think that she gets a lot of that from, you know, from the journal idea of being able to put down her thoughts when she can't necessarily put them together verbally to be able to say, "Mommy this is what's going on."

Families grow together

In their helpful book for parents and other caregivers, *Family Storybook Reading,* Denny Taylor and Dorothy Strickland (1986) wrote:

> Family storybook reading is a special time when families grow together, as parents and children learn about one another and the world in which they live. . . . When parents read stories to their children they are creating a safe, warm place for language and literacy learning. . . . Exposed to loving and caring human beings as reading models, children demonstrate an ever-increasing interest in books and stories as well as in the masses of print that surround them in their environment. Most important, they begin to view themselves as becoming readers and writers too. (pp. 5–6)

This "safe, warm" time together, as we have seen, was a time as much for talk as for text. Book stories sometimes led to family stories. At a parent meeting Cathy's mother explained that after her child read with her, she often asked for a family story:

> Have you got a story about a book like this or has something like this happened to you? I mean, at bath time we're in there going, "Tell me a story about . . . ," and it's all because of all the expressions they used, I feel like, in the journal, and, you know, in the reading. I mean, it makes me think, you know, I ought to write this stuff down. I really should because, you know, my parents aren't here now, you know, but at least I have this stuff that I could . . . All the time she says, Do you have a story about . . .

This was one of the many meaningful and varied ways that literature enriched these families' lives. We already knew how connected each family was, how each parent (or other family member) who wrote described the child as "special" and "loved." Reading books; talking about events, characters, morals, and personal connections; and writing or drawing these responses gave families a way to make their connectedness concrete. They have these journals in their homes now, as reminders of a special time in their children's lives, a time when they shared the joy of emergent literacy and the wonder of children's literature.

NINE
Child-Teacher Connections

One of the strongest features of our day-to-day correspondence was the personal connections we established with students. In writing her own history as a learner, one who had loved school, JoBeth realized that it was really the personal relationships she had with certain teachers that had been most meaningful. Her significant memories almost always involved dialogues with teachers who treated her as though she were someone worth talking to. She was respected. What she had to say mattered. The journals provided a point of development for this kind of relationship building for Betty and Barbara and their students.

Building personal relationships

Gavin's journal was a wonderful example of this kind of direct and personal relationship building. He often asked Betty questions about her life outside of school. Once he wondered in writing what her house was made of, and when Betty responded that her house was made of wood, he reassured her with a literary connection that "a Big Bad wlf won't come a Big Wolf can not Blow a wood House Down." He also inquired about Betty's ability to climb trees, and even asked, "Are you in love?" She took each question seriously and answered just as if Barbara or JoBeth had been the nosey one.

On one occasion Gavin wrote to Betty for reassurance that he could develop a partnership with just her if need be: "I didn't got To Rit I did my book at school and Ms. Shockley I Red Why Dog Hate Cat Then I Just looked at the pictures My mom was Sleep I Hope I Did Good The end" For Gavin, as for others, there wasn't a family member involved in the writing each time. For some families, obvious involvement was sporadic, whereas for others it seemed to be a treasured time that was rarely missed. But for the children, no matter what the home situation might have been day to day, the journals remained a dependable link to another responsive adult—their classroom teacher.

A parent shared with us how much her child valued the teacher's personal attention in the journals:

> I mean, I think it's a good form of expression there, too, because it's another kind of dialogue with an adult that, you know, you say back relatively adult things and you all are still communicating, you know, and I think that she thinks that's really neat. I mean, she has your attention, you know, for that . . . for whatever she writes, even if it's silly, you know. . . . You respond to it. You respond to it even if it's something silly

or if it's something very deep that she needed to say about something, you know, you respond to it no matter what.

An unexpected bonus of the journal writing was the increased visibility of children who were rather shy or who for some other reason did not stand out during the regular school day. This was particularly true for Torrey. His journal helped Betty see beyond the quiet, shy child who rarely spoke in class to the more complex view his mother shared in her journal writing. His mother's belief in him, and her pleasure at the progress she saw, worked to assure Betty that from his mother's perspective, Torrey was making progress and doing well as a reader. Her most frequent comments were generally evaluative: "He continues to do great in his reading," or "His progress continues to magnify." Torrey's mom was a strong advocate for her son, and her insights served to keep Torrey's accomplishments continually in sight. At the beginning of first grade, in response to the "tell me about your child" letter, his mom wrote,

> He is a gentle, sweet, but shy person. He is eager to learn. But his shyness hinders his abilities at times. . . . His confidence in hisself is not the greatest. However, he will overcome this with Love and attention.

She was right, and her explicit insight helped us get to know Torrey better and sooner than we might have otherwise. The understanding and support paid dividends. We were all excited when his mother exclaimed:

> Torrey really surprised me tonight. He read to me "Zack's Alligator." A book I just knew was to advance for him. He never fails to amaze me. You have done a marvelous job teaching him this school year. My son has made *great* progress. You are a great teacher!!! May God bless you, Joyce. (3-2-92)

Torrey came alive on the journal pages in a way that he often did not in the classroom, and his relationships with his teachers both at home and at school were certainly strengthened by this extended form of relationship building.

Renee's was a similar story. In her second-grade response to the "tell me about your child" letter, her mother wrote much the same thing she had shared in first grade: "Renee is a sweet little girl, she gets along with everyone once she get to know them, at first she's very shy, she likes to learn different things." In fact, she was so quiet and shy Betty worried about not giving her the kind of attention she might need, because Renee rarely asked for help or called attention to herself in any way. Journal responses such as the following series from several members of Renee's extended family added to Betty's understanding of the child:

> Renee decided to go into her own "little world" tonight. We still completed it. J. Miller [mother's friend]

> Renee read very well, but some of the words were a little hard but we finished the book. Linda Morris [mother]

> Renee did very well. She had trouble with some words. She finish the book. She was naughty, a little. Catuma Garey [cousin]

Our picture of Renee filled out when we viewed her through her family's eyes, not just as a "behaving student."

Teachers sometimes used characters, events, or issues in books the children were reading to provide social or emotional support as they developed deeper relationships of trust. Barbara helped Chris address his emerging role in the classroom community, where he seemed out of place and felt unliked. The other kids thought he was "wimpy" because he cried often. When he read a ghost story, he wrote, "The boy wasn't afraid of nothing." Barbara wrote back, "What a brave boy! Some people think you are just as brave because you are not scared of bugs and little animals." Soon after, she responded to Chris's entry about a "very very mean" witch who kicks people: "Chris, I was glad when they kicked her back—were you? When they worked together they took care of their problem. That happens in real life too." Through journal writing Chris was able to see himself through the eyes of another adult who could stress his talents in the context of a shared history.

Supporting literacy development: some things take time to grow

The journals gave teachers a window on children's literacy development and a chance to respond sensitively to individual needs as they supported children's emerging concepts. In second grade Dumoneak wrote about *The Boxcar Children*:

> I like the frist and Second chapter I like the frist chapter because it was funny it was funny because grandfather got sick. but it was sad too . . . I like the second Chapter because it was funny too. I like the sixth I got to go!

Barbara realized that Dumoneak may not have understood the structure of this new kind of book, and wrote,

> Did you know that a chapter book is different from a big book with a lot of stories in it? In a chapter book there is one long story. So start with Chapter 1 and read a little every day until you get to the end of the story. You will probably need a bookmark. Ms. M

Relationships were close and personal. Teachers and students were able to respond to one another as individuals. This kind of response is so different from a "second graders should be able to" perspective. The preceding example shows how Barbara was able to relate to Dumoneak's specific needs as an individual learner.

Literacy development is much more than decoding or even comprehending. Members of a reading community have certain responsibilities. We observed that journal conversations increasingly became reader-to-reader rather than teacher-to-child. In October of second grade Colin wrote to Barbara, "I know I'm not supposed to tell you, but White Bird dies." An unspoken rule in a community of readers is that you don't "give away" a great plot; but sometimes stories are just too good *not* to talk about. In their small adult reading community Barbara, JoBeth, and Betty experienced a similar moment when they had tried to discuss Barbara Kingsolver's novel *Pigs in Heaven*. Betty had just finished it, Barbara was two thirds of the way through, and JoBeth was close behind. As Betty tried to find out where the other two readers were, she and Barbara disclosed some information that JoBeth had not yet read. "Don't tell me any more!" she begged.

The communication between child, parent, and teacher gave us many opportunities to help the children grow as responders. We did not push, but nudged, and we did it periodically throughout the year, hoping each time that the child had developed to a point where s/he could benefit from the suggestion. We used a variety of approaches, from directly stated requests to modeling.

For example, Cathy not only modeled her writing after teacher entries but also responded immediately to teacher requests. Betty wrote, "Your responses are very nice. Could you try to remember to use punctuation marks now?" In the next entry Cathy included punctuation marks and continued to use them in almost every response throughout the first and second grades.

Not all the students were so receptive to our suggestions. We found what every teacher knows: sometimes, no matter how you present something, the child just does not make the hoped-for change. Some children seemed to ignore requests and suggestions, yet weeks later they would change their responses, reflecting the influence of the teacher's earlier comments or suggestions on their writing.

For example, Ashley had a firm sense of what her journal entries should be like. Every entry began with "This book is about," followed by a short synopsis of the story. Betty asked questions and modeled more extended responses to the books. Ashley ignored her questions. After months of this type of exchange, Betty wrote, "What else did you think about this book?" and "Tell me more." When there was no change, she wrote to Ashley, "You do such a good job telling me what your books are about. I would like for you to also write about how the book made you feel and what made it interesting." Ashley did not respond to this directive. Finally, Betty broke down and begged, "Come on, Ashley . . . Please tell me more about the books you read." The next entry Ashley added a "What I like about this story" section to her standard review format. She continued this patterned response throughout first grade. In second grade her entries were more personal. She wrote about parts of the books that she liked, told why she liked them, and made many connections to life in the classroom.

Some things just take time to grow. Since we were able to observe Ashley and her classmates over two years, we had a perspective that it is hard to acquire in one school year. What a delight it was to see what grew when we gave the children time to develop in individual ways, at individual paces, for two years in classrooms similar in philosophy. Children who would have been left behind at the end of first grade blossomed when they were able to stay with a familiar and supportive community of learners in second grade. Shy children were able to adjust quickly to second grade and take their places as contributors to the group.

The ongoing information about the individual student's literacy development that Betty compiled in first grade informed Barbara in second grade. This shared information gave her a broader perspective of each child's growth and influenced the kind of support she offered to the children as they continued to develop in second grade. This longer-range look at each child also allowed us to see clearly the individual patterns of growth—the starts, stops, and growth spurts that were unique to each student. Providing the children time to grow allowed many students whose timetable for learning was different from the basal program's or the grade-level scope and sequence chart to be successful in school.

"Meet me at write-in time": seeing teachers as writers

Children too rarely see their teachers as "real" writers; both the journals and the writing workshop gave us opportunities to take that role. In the journals children saw us as adults who read and responded to literature, who liked to talk about books with children and adults, and who wrote to understand themselves and others. In writing workshop children saw us as people who wrote for pleasure, to entertain others, and to express emotions. In short, students saw teachers at home and at school using writing for a variety of real-life purposes. As Peterson (1992) pointed out,

> Holistic teachers try to create learning situations that are connected to life. . . . Life activities are not reading to answer schoolbook questions at the end of a chapter or practicing to improve scores on an achievement test, but are what people do in real life. When we are involved with life activities we plan and complete joint projects, collaborate, negotiate meaning, view our own and the work of others from a critical perspective, [and] care for others. (p. 128)

Betty and Barbara wrote for all these purposes, and the students viewed them as writers. Children periodically asked their teachers to join them as co-authors, with the journals providing a planning link between student and teacher. These invitations were issued both by the child to the teacher and by the teacher to the child. In one case, Renee shared her interest in a long-term effort with Barbara:

> *Hail to the Chief.* I read a Joke Book it was funny I laugh at funny this is a Joke for you you can lagh at it I like to write maybe when I be grownup I mit be a teach then we can write a sory to gether.

Barbara responded with enthusiasm:

> Renee—maybe we can write a story together before you are grown. It may be too long for me to wait until you are grown. (1/22/93)

Renee saw herself as a writer, and she saw her teacher as a writer. She would like to be a teacher when she grows up, and as a teacher, chances are good that she will also be a writer.

On another occasion Betty issued the initial invitation and Gavin wrote back, "Yes we can write A Book Meet Me At Writein Time and we can write a Book." One parent even noticed the effect on her child. Cathy's mom reported to us, "She has become a very good writer. She writes with a lot of detail. She would like to be an author. Like her teachers."

The journals connected us with children in a deeper, more continuous way than we have ever experienced before. As children like Renee wrote with their teachers, and children like Colin included teachers in their response communities, they came to understand that you don't have to be a grown-up to participate fully in a literate community. You get to be who you are and learn to hope for a friend to share it all with you.

TEN
Reader-Book Connections

Sara danced into the classroom one chilly February morning, clutching a book to her heart. She asked urgently, "Ms. Shockley, can I read *Fox Went out on a Chilly Night* to the class? Every single night I get in bed and hug that book and start singing it!"

In *Talking About Books* (Short and Pierce, 1990), teachers of kindergarten through college-age students encouraged readers in their classes to engage in literate talk about literature. As these teachers observed and reflected on the literacy communities that developed, they identified many of the ways readers benefit from extended discussions about books. Through reading good literature and talking about it with other readers, students connected with other people and other cultures, journeyed to other worlds, developed their imaginations, internalized new words and meanings, developed a sense of various text structures and language patterns, and became what Frank Smith (1988) called "members of the literacy club": people who choose to read and write.

Charlotte Huck (1990), an expert on books and the children who read them, stresses that literature has the power to transform, to make the reader more fully human. To be more fully human often means falling in love, as Sara did with her book, and as countless other children have done. It may also mean examining one's own life in relation to book lives and exploring relationships among authors, illustrators, and characters.

Betty's reader-book connection

Being teachers who are also readers and writers made a difference for each of us. Educators such as Nancie Atwell, Carol Avery, Donald Graves, and Lucy Calkins have encouraged teachers to "discover your own literacy" (Graves, 1990), but many teachers haven't yet realized the valuable link. Betty lived it. The following section presents excerpts from her reading autobiography.

Becoming real

Entering my childhood home had an immediate literary impact. My mother planned it that way. She knew that books were a symbol of knowing and caring, and she made this statement with an architecturally pleasing wall of built-in bookshelves placed strategically in view of anyone who opened the door. Mother joined a book club as soon as she and Dad decided to build the house.

The thing was, I never once saw my mother or anyone else actually reading those books. To this day, the books remain unchanged and unchallenged, the E. B. White shelf fenced by the hand-painted teapot bookend, third shelf up on the right.

My younger years were not totally devoid of literary enticements. I know that my writing style can be directly linked to my mother's prolific letter writing. I never went anywhere for more than one night that I didn't find a letter waiting for me when I arrived. Mother loved words and used them cleverly. And although I don't remember bedtime stories, I do have a strong sense of story connected with my father and his ability to tell a tale or a joke with remarkable timing and sense of audience.

I knew that reading was supposed to be a good thing, but my home experience and the lackluster texts and dreary reading groups of school had not made me believe it. When, as a teacher, I saw children being taught to read in the same way, dissociated from real life, I was ready to make a change.

That metamorphosis did not begin until I was thirty-eight. That year JoBeth was a co-researcher in my room, and through her I discovered that it was possible to love books, to need books, to savor language, to use and play with words, and to make my own literacy an integral part of my life. For my thirty-ninth birthday JoBeth gave me three books by Lee Smith. That was the first time anyone had ever given me a book as a gift.

Now I share books, give books, and treat myself to books every chance I get. I have bookshelves at my house now, but they are not built-in; they are free-standing. They mark a newfound freedom to let my living count through text and to live other lives through text, especially my growing collection of personal narratives. Books are for real now, not just for appearance's sake.

Teachers who are readers

Before she came to know herself as a reader and writer, Betty was a good teacher. In fact, she was first runner-up for state teacher of the year. The first thing she composed outside of required college writing was the detailed and reflective analysis of her teaching required for that honor. Even as she was being recognized in such a public way for her teaching, Betty knew there was a big difference between the way she supported her students as readers and writers then and the way she escorted them to literacy when she became a reader and writer herself. Teachers, by making their literacy trials and triumphs explicit to themselves and to their students, connect learner-to-learner.

Families recognized this different stance, the shift from Teacher as Answer Woman to Teacher as Learner. After participating with us during the two years of our study, several parents told us we had become more like real people in their eyes, not just "the teacher." This increased realness, achieved by building oral and written connections with families, was felt also by Betty when she began to understand herself as a whole language teacher. One of her first changes in practice was to teach herself about children's literature by doing author studies with her students. As they learned about the people who wrote the books, she came to see authors as people who could live down the street, not as inimitable literary icons. She presented these authors to her students in this new light, telling stories about what a long time it had taken Peter Spier to get to school every day, and how when he was their age Donald Crews really did go to Big Mama's house for summer vacations.

As Betty explored these connections in the classroom, she also recognized them in her own reading. Often choosing to read literature written by Southerners, she began to make friendly literary associations with writers from Chapel Hill, where she had completed her undergraduate degree. She could picture Clyde Edgerton and Lee Smith having Sunday brunch at the Carolina Coffee Shop. She brought Georgia writers to life for her students by sharing from books she read by writers such as Terry Kay, Raymond Andrews, Tina Ansa, Ann Rivers Siddons, Pat Conroy, and Melissa Fay Greene.

At the time of this writing, Betty was reading a book by Ruthie Bolton, as told to Josephine Humphreys. Humphreys introduced Bolton's oral narrative thus:

> Ruthie Bolton and I call the same place home: Charleston and its islands, some of which are bodies of land surrounded by water and some of which are clusters of people divided by less bridgeable things. We were both born and raised here, and live not ten minutes apart, but we never met until the summer of 1993.

Stories bridge "less bridgeable things." When we as writers, young or old, read with friendly authors and write for friendly audiences, we begin to see ourselves as active constructors of the literary world rather than as decoders on demand. We read and write differently when there are possibilities for us in the process. Reading becomes a way to rehearse new lives for ourselves, and writing becomes a way to represent those lives fictionally or realistically, as Carolyn Heilbrun (1988) explained in *Writing a Woman's Life*. We teachers are readers and writers; we watched with joy and awe as children and families read and wrote their lives.

Personal connections to stories

It was exciting, as a day-to-day event, to see the children make personal connections to the books they read. It was not until we analyzed each child's responses over time that we realized the depth and breadth of some of these connections.

Renee's second-grade journal was almost all personal connections to books. She told what she would do, or wished for a similar situation, or described her response ("It made me laugh"). She really put herself into the book world, often thinking of how she would do things differently than the book characters. In her entry for *No Bath Tonight*, she said, "If I had that many hurts, I would give it some air, then I will put the bandaide on" (12/14).

Kimberly, a child who had copied parts of books in her journal for almost all of first grade, began making personal connections to the books she was reading at the very beginning of second grade:

> *Who Will Be My Mother?*   I would be sad if I didn't have my mother. (9/11)

> *Down by the Bay*   They was keep saying did you ever see a whale? I saw a whale when I was in Canada at the seaworld last year. (11/30)

> *Cam Jansen*   I like the dinosaur bones I went to the Frnhrbdt [Fernbank] and I saw some Dinosaur Bones and dfen caing [friends came] to The And. (1/19)

Kim did most of the responding in her journal. One night her mother participated by posing a question for Kim, as shown in the next example. We imagine that on many other nights discussing books with her family encouraged Kimberly to make the personal connections that she shared in her journal.

Kim: Fox On the Job—The fox wanted a job to get some money to buy him a bike.
Mom: Kim, do you have to get a job to buy your bike?
Kim: No, and my mom and my father by my bike.

The questions Kimberly's teachers included in their journal responses may also have influenced Kim's entries and family discussions. Frequently, these teacher responses included not only questions but personal connections to the books the children were writing about:

Kim: Clifford the Red Dog—I like clifford he is read and he do any thieg I love clifford
Barbara: Would you like to have a huge dog like Clifford? He is sweet, but I might be afraid of such a big dog. Would you? Ms. M.

Although many of the children made personal connections to the books they read, others did not. For months in second grade Chris wrote short synopses of the books he read. Barbara asked questions and modeled her own personal connections to encourage a more thoughtful response. After reading a book about a class that had a cat as a pet, Chris finally wrote a response that was very personal. "Critter the class cat The cat is funny. And can we have a cat? I will name it" (3/30/93). He even pursued his desire to have a class cat by writing a letter to the principal, asking her permission to have a cat at school. He was quite disappointed when Dr. Denero vetoed the class-cat plan.

Ashley was another student who seemed reluctant to change her journal responses. In second grade she continued the summaries that had been her standard in first grade. Barbara told her about other books, suggested book connections, and asked her questions that encouraged personal-textual connections. For example, on October 13, Barbara wrote, "Ashley, Do you think that could really happen? Have you ever read any other stories where an animal ate a person and then the person got out of the animal? I'm thinking of one—can you?" Ashley did not respond. On November 5, Barbara wrote:

Does this story remind you of being in a play? Tonight when you write about the book you read, try to think of how it makes you feel—or something it makes *you* think of. Then write to me about one of those things.

Ashley almost never responded directly or immediately, even to these directives. It would have been easy to get frustrated or discouraged. But Ashley eventually grew into one of the most reflective, connected readers in the class.

In second grade she reread and responded to a book that had been a favorite in first grade, *The Talking Eggs:*

I like this book because the mom and sister did not want that water and the little girl got mad and ran away for a little while. I was mad because they was doing that little girl wrong and that old woman and the girl went to the city.

Contrast that with her first-grade response to the same book: "This is about a little girl getting lots of pretty stuff."

Ashley's reaction (February, second grade) to *Possum Come a-Knockin'* included her peers' responses and a thoughtful reference to a character the class had assumed was a boy: "I like this book because it has a possum knocked on the door, and all the people

in our class think cussin is a bad werd. And I like the baby, because she or he is cute."
She read *The Very Hungry Caterpillar* in May of second grade and wrote:

> I like this book because it is good. and his illustrations too. he youse tarn paper crauns and marer [used torn paper, crayons, and markers] and he relly puts you in the story. Like Jone Sceesca [John Scieszka]

All the suggesting, modeling, directing, and begging came to fruition, but Ashley (like *Leo the Late Bloomer*) bloomed in her own good time.

At times, it was the parents who made personal connections to the stories they read with their children. At other times, parent and child shared their personal reflections about the books. Brad and his mother, Pam, wrote the following in second grade:

> This [*Strega Nona*] is very different from the other stories that Brad brings home. I haven't read a story about a witch in many years. At least Strega Nona was a kind and helpful witch. In most stories for children, the witches are terrible. Pam J.
>
> *Jackie Robinson*, Chapter 1 The Freedom Train. The first chapter was well written and interesting. Its strange to read about the struggles of Black people that are still being fought today almost 50 years after Jackie Robinson was born. It makes me sad but I enjoy reading about famous contributions of Black Americans. Pam J.

Brad's response was "Jackie Robinson lived in Georgia like me." Both mother and son really connected with this book, one for the social issues, the other by seeing something he had in common with a famous person.

Book-to-book connections

Another type of connection we saw these young readers make was between different books they had read. Colin was one child who began comparing books in first grade, often when reading with his mother (and probably with her guidance). From the start of second grade he wrote about the connections he saw between books he was currently reading and books he remembered. The connections he shared were about content and illustrations.

In first grade Colin listed similarities and differences he noticed when comparing the classroom version of Pecos Bill to a version of the story from his home book collection. He also shared his insights about a book that was a spin-off of *The Emperor's New Clothes*:

> *The Principal's New Clothes* by Stephanie Calmenson I like it because it's silly and it's got good pictures. My favorite character is Moe because he's silly. Sometimes people play with words, but this time the author played with a story. This story is like The Emperor's New Clothes. (9/25/91)

From the very first journal entry in second grade Colin made connections between books. He continued to do this throughout the year. Whereas in first grade he and his mother often responded together, in second grade Colin wrote almost all his own responses:

George and Martha Rise and Shine by James Marshall   I chose this book because I like the author. I thout it would be funny but it isn't I used to like this kind of book but I do not anymore. (9/8)

Rapscallion Jones by James Marshall   I piked this book because I have read a lot of fox books. the drawings look different. He looks like a older fox. (9/14)

My Place in Space by Robin and Sally Hirst   This book is like a Waldo book because all the little details in the illustrations. (9/24)

Jokes from the crypt by Eleanor Fremont Illustrations by Aristides Ruiz   The books cover illustration is done by one of the artists of Mad. His name is jack Davis. It is dedicated to William M. Gaines. He made up Mad. (11/3)

The Not So Jolly Roger by Jon Scieszka   These books are great !!!!!!! I can not wate till I get my nxt book! Fred is not smart in this book like he is in the first book. (3/30)

Frequently, we responded to a child's journal by making a connection to another book. We modeled responses to literature in classroom discussions as well as in the journals. As we shared connections we made among class read-alouds, our adult pleasure reading, and student independent reading choices, we encouraged students to see connections among the books they read (including the ones they wrote themselves). We suggested related books to read throughout the year:

Ashley: *The old Woman who lived in a vinegar Bottle* this is about a woman who lived in a jug and she met a funny looking late [lady]. (9/20)
Barbara: *The Old Woman Who Lived in a Vinegar Bottle* is one of my favorite stories. Boy, she isn't happy with anything! She just wants more, more, more. Have you read *The Magic Fish?* We have it at the listening center. The Fisherman's wife is kinda like the old lady. I think you'd like it! Ms. M.

Connecting books, or intertextuality, develops as children read and discuss books in a supportive social context (Cullinan and Galda 1994). Not all our students made such connections, and most did so rather infrequently. However, with so many books, and so many people talking about and relating books, we suspect these readers were nudged into more mature response patterns.

Illustrations as connections

Illustrations were an important way some children connected to books. Many children (and one parent) included illustrations in their journal responses. For example, Ashley almost always summarized her books with a picture as well as with a narrative. Usually she drew a representative scene (Figure 10-1) or a favorite character. However, when she wrote about how sad *The Clown of God* (DePaola) made her, she drew herself (Figure 10-2).

Brad's mom shared a glimpse into their home reading time when she and Brad wrote the following response in second grade:

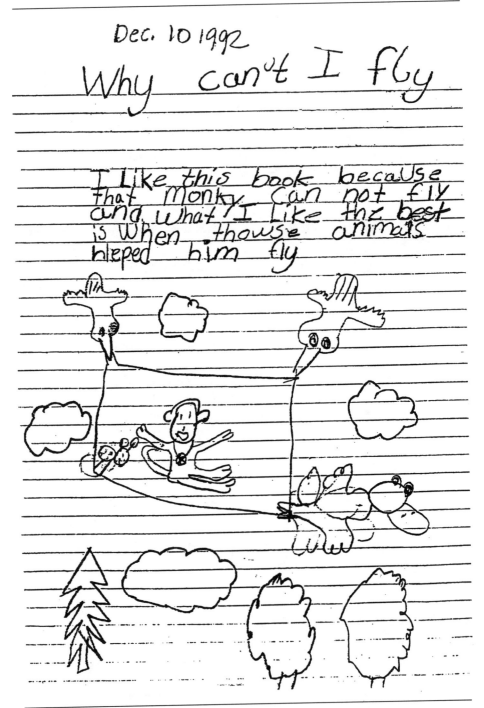

Dec. 10 1992

Why can't I fly

I like this book because
that monky can not fly
and what I like the best
is when thowse animals
hleped him fly

FIG. 10-1   *Ashley's picture for* Why Can't I Fly?

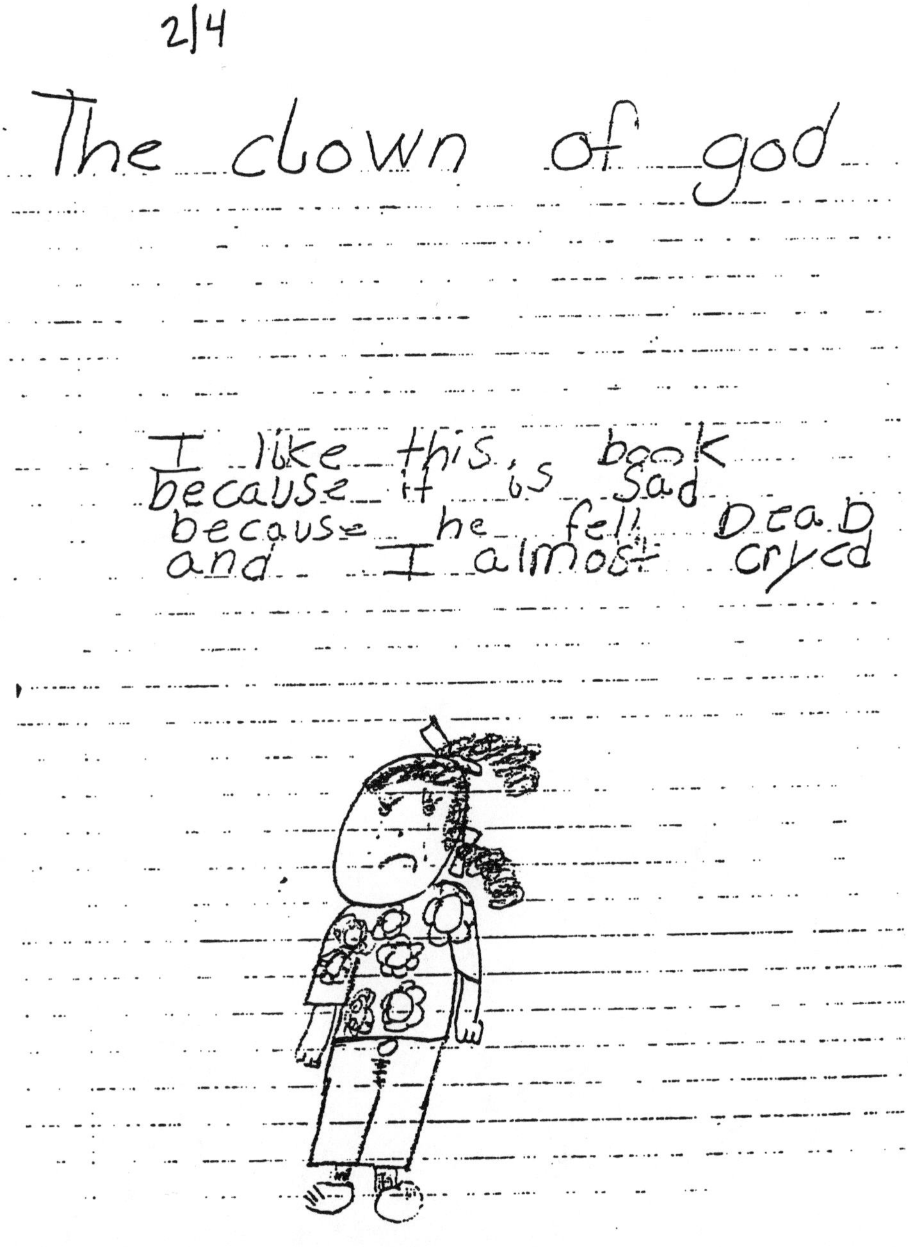

2|4

The clown of god

I like this book
because it is sad
because he fell DeaD
and I almost cryed

FIG. 10-2   *Ashley's picture for* The Clown of God

Brian: The biggest house in the world. if the snail was stronger he would be able to carry the house. Brad

Mom: Brad came to an interesting conclusion. I thought it was illustrated beautifully and I pointed out to Brad the fact the author also wrote "Tillie and the Wall." He agreed, he remembered the name, Leo Lionni. Pam Johnson

Brad was quite an artist. He had created some comic book type of characters that he used in illustrating many of the stories he wrote. Brad clearly expressed his love for comics when he wrote, "The Punisher it was the greatest I ever read. It had chapters in it. It had lots of action in i t. I like this sort of comics." Betty encouraged Brad to share his own comic drawings with a wider audience. At the beginning of second grade his mother wrote to Barbara:

A little something extra about Brad is a wonderful experience that he had over the summer. He sent a letter and a few drawings to Marvel Comics. They replied thanking him and sending a free comic book not yet at the stores. This was wonderfull because he thought of writing the company, and they were great in responding to him by letter, which encouraged him to write. Pam Johnson

Each reader found his or her own way to respond to books. We encouraged and praised them, while nudging them to grow in their reading and writing abilities. The journals provided a place for their efforts to be acknowledged and their individual voices to be heard.

ISSUES OF POLICY AND PRACTICE

ELEVEN

Partnerships, Not Programs

Programs are implemented; partnerships are developed. Programs are adopted; partnerships are constructed. Parent involvement programs as America's schools have implemented them have serious problems. By their very nature, most programs have steps, elements, or procedures that become static. A program cannot constantly reinvent itself, change with each year, be different in every classroom, and for every teacher-family-child relationship. Yet schools and parents have a shared and vested interest in children that almost demands some kind of collaboration. We believe, along with an increasing number of home and school educators, that this shared responsibility should be a genuine partnership.

Reexamining parent involvement programs (PIPS)

David Dillon (1989, p. 8) decried the inappropriate nature of most PIPS, which are often touted as collaborations but in fact are not:

> At lots of meetings of parents . . . the anxiety that parents have about their children's developing literacy, their own insecurity about their ability to help them are palpable. . . . And when the literacy experts go ahead . . . and tell parents what to do (apparently assuming the parents don't know it and aren't doing it), they do little to dispel the parents' anxiety and insecurity. In fact, they may well increase it, confirming parents' tendencies not to trust themselves. The hidden message I see in such discourse is that we don't think much of parents' abilities.

Programs are problematic in several ways. Aspects of PIPS often become generalized rather than being specific to classroom or family interests or needs. Most often, PIPS are the only way the school recognizes parents as people who should also be involved in the education of their children. And in most programs, the only parents who get recognized are the ones who participate—on the school's terms. Such programs are intended to be adopted systematically, and schools often buy into them as a whole.

In the evaluation of parent involvement programs, schools ask, "Did we do it right?" The measure of most programs is the physical presence of parents in the school at PTO meetings, parent-teacher conferences, or as classroom volunteers or teacher aides doing what teachers ask of them; or the physical evidence that parents did something at school-like home such as signing a behavior contract or a homework sheet, reading for a certain number of minutes, or agreeing to pay for lost books. Such

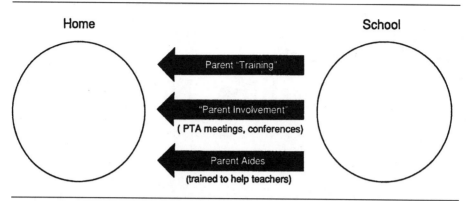

FIG. 11-1   *One-way Models of Parent Involvement*

projects often seek to "train" parents in the ways of the school and mainstream society, and they assume a home-deficit approach. Policy analysts McLaughlin and Shields (1987), noting that parents with low incomes are often seen by schools as less involved, found that most parental involvement programs defined involvement *on the school's terms* and often favored parents with the time and money to do volunteer work in the schools. These attempts, though well meaning, are most often limited by their under-lying belief that parents should change or should give something to the school; few facilitate a two-way interaction between home and school (see Figure 11-1).

Problems with PIPS are often exacerbated in low-income communities. McLaughlin and Shields (1987) reported:

> Such school-based programs have tended to engage the participation of advantaged parents, but not of low-income parents. In those locales in which parent-involvement strategies have successfully promoted the participation of low-income parents, how-ever, there is considerable evidence that the expected benefits actually accrue. (p. 157)

Unfortunately, few parent involvement programs invite either teachers or fam-ilies to participate in program development. The school either did the program right or wrong, good parents participated and not-so-good parents didn't, and the responsi-bility lay primarily with one person—the principal or a parent involvement program coordinator.

Home-school partnerships

In contrast, partnerships develop. A genuine partnership is constructed jointly by all the participants. Each participant has the responsibility to commit to both individual and shared goals. Rather than growing bigger, in terms of more people doing the same program, partnerships grow more intimate. Rather than stabilizing into set program elements, partnerships remain unstable and dynamic, changing with the needs of any member. There is no right way to develop a partnership because that would imply a single model. There is a constant negotiation of the relationship. Families have oppor-tunities to share with teachers their routines, values, and issues, just as teachers have

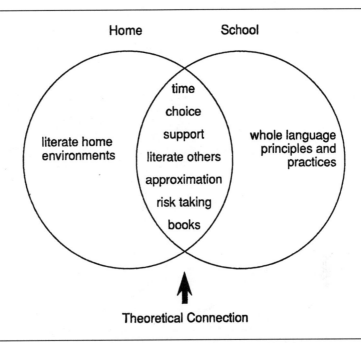

Home   School

time

choice

literate home   support   whole language
environments   literate others   principles and
                                          practices
approximation

risk taking

books

Theoretical Connection

FIG. 11-2   *Theoretical Connection Between Home and School*

the opportunity to share with families classroom routines, values, and issues. Mc-
Laughlin and Shields (1987) concluded:

> The development and support of effective parent-involvement strategies hinges on local
> realities and on the attitudes and beliefs of those individuals who are primarily respon-
> sible for the implementation of such strategies.

In other words, the more local (as in one teacher to each family individually) and the
more respectful and knowledgeable we as teachers are about family attitudes and beliefs
(and vice versa), the more effective our efforts on behalf of children are likely to be.

As whole language teachers in the years before this study, we only hoped that we
had this kind of shared beliefs with families. In fact, we had only created a theoretical
connection between home and school (see Figure 11-2). Whole language theory and
practice are built upon studies of what goes on in literate family environments, where
children listen to favorite books over and over, are supported in their own emergent
literacy and encouraged to "invent" reading and writing, and see others using literacy
for meaningful purposes on a daily basis. *Engaging Children* taught us that we were
assuming too much of that theoretical connection, that we had much more to learn from
families.

Jointly constructed parallel practices have the potential, which we believe for the
families in our classrooms was realized (see Figure 11-3), for what researcher Susan
Swap (1993) calls a partnership model. Based on her research, she feels partnerships
hold the most promise for transforming, rather than transmitting, knowledge. She calls
for partnerships that encompass "long-term commitments, mutual respect, widespread
involvement . . . , and sharing of planning and decision-making responsibilities"

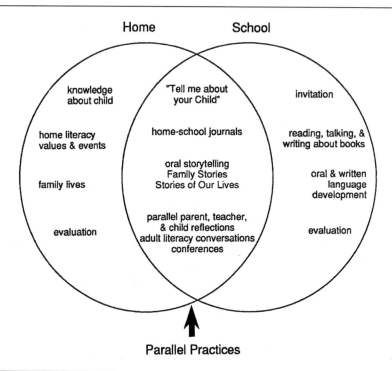

Home   School

knowledge
about child

"Tell me about
your Child"

invitation

home literacy
values & events

home-school journals

reading, talking, &
writing about books

oral storytelling
Family Stories
Stories of Our Lives

family lives

oral & written
language
development

parallel parent, teacher,
& child reflections
adult literacy conversations
conferences

evaluation

evaluation

Parallel Practices

FIG. 11-3   *Extending Literacy Community: A Home-School Partnership*

(p. 46). She and other researchers who examine home-school connections found a
positive link between some, but not all, parent involvement attempts and student
success in school. When the programs contributed to student success, parents knew that
what they were doing was meaningful, saw direct benefits for their children, felt that
schools were committed to them as parents, and knew that their involvement made a
difference.

In developing our partnerships with families, we were not trying to impose our
vision of literacy but to develop relationships with families where we could learn about
what already existed in the families and connect that with the literacy classroom
community. We were trying to learn from parents what literacy events were important
in their lives and share with them the important literacy events in their children's
school. We recognized that families as well as teachers have busy lives. We needed
channels for developing meaningful partnerships that were open, dependable, nonintru-
sive and nonevaluative. As parents ourselves, we had been in the position of the parents
of our students. We felt we had information about our children that would have helped
their teachers understand and teach our children better.

The partnerships we formed with families gave tremendous support to all the adults
who had the profound responsibility of nurturing a child. The teachers no longer felt
solely accountable for the children's learning. They received encouragement and important new insights from the families and the children. The families had a way back
into the system of school that many had left with less-than-fond memories. They knew
their efforts were both helpful and appreciated. The children saw their parents and their
teachers working together, sharing, and caring about them. Most important, we all found

we wanted the best for each child, even when we had different ways of approaching literacy.

Were we, as David Dillon worried, "co-opting" or "exploiting" these parents, "turning the home into an extension of the classroom" (1989, p. 9)? Were we "pushing an instructional approach," namely whole language? We don't believe so. What we offered and valued were individualized responses to a set of practices that we saw as pathways to partnership. We acted at the classroom level and tried to create a meaningful match between home and school, one home at a time. The gathering of these matches did as much for the classroom community as it did for each family-teacher-child triad. As Belenky et al. (1986) wrote:

> Each of us has a unique perspective that is in some sense irrefutably "right" by virtue of its existence. But the connected class transforms these private truths into "objects," publicly available to the members of the class who, through "stretching and sharing," add to themselves as knowers by absorbing in their own fashion their classmates' [and families'] ideas. (p. 223)

The process we initiated was realistic, manageable, and meaningful for us, for children, and for families. It was a particular effort for a particular place. Instead of "co-opting," we saw ourselves as fostering each other's expertise.

Foundations and consequences

Respect and belief in family knowledge and caring are our core values; we based partnership decisions and actions on these values. We believed that families had important knowledge to add to ours. We respected and used what was offered. We believed there was no one right way to respond to literature or write a family story. We respected what was offered and celebrated it with their children. We believed parents cared, and we offered a way to reenter schooling without requiring they be physically present for a roll call of good parents. We respected what they offered and thanked them often for the time and effort they shared with us and their children. They, in turn, treated us with respect and thanked us on behalf of their children.

These elements of trust, shared goals, and genuine dialogue on a regular basis were critical to each child's supported growth. Bronfenbrenner (1979) proposed that development is facilitated when there are linkages between the settings that "encourage the development of mutual trust, a positive orientation, goal consensus between settings, and an evolving balance of power responsive to action in behalf of the developing person" (p. 216). Additionally, he hypothesized that development is facilitated when there is a two-way communication between the settings, and "valid information, advice, and experience relevant to one setting are made available, on a continuing basis, to the other" (p. 217). The partnerships the families created with us were established on the parents' terms rather than those of the school, although we issued the invitations.

We recognized that what Vygotsky (1978) called the socially constructed nature of knowledge occurred through our invitations to partnership. Vygotsky's notion of the influence of social, historical, and cultural contexts influenced individual responses and interactions. We noted the effects of previous school and home experiences (those of the parent, the child, and the teacher), family values, and family circumstances. The parallel practices of "tell me about your child," reader response journals, family storybook writing, shared reflections, and family meetings became meaningful ways to construct shared understandings with parents as we interacted with each other about what children should learn and how they should learn it.

We interpreted the 100 percent participation of these families over a period of two years as confirming Sattes' conclusions in her 1985 review: "Parent involvement impacts student achievement when that involvement is meaningful to parents" (p. 11). The journals represented a real connection between home and school. Everyone came to depend on and use the mutual access they represented.

Our close involvement with these children and their families taught us about the need to respect and support, not undermine, the assistance that families offer their children. In some situations, teachers react negatively to what they perceive to be "dangerous" interventions by parents. They advise parents, "Just read with your children and leave the teaching to us." For example, if a parent required a child to spell words from the text in a response journal, some teachers would be very uncomfortable with this practice for an emergent reader. However, we found it was important to understand and support this parent's approach to helping the child. Sometimes we shared with parents other ways of interacting, but we never expressed disagreement with their decisions. When one family member decided to read Bible stories to Renee instead of having her read the book she brought home from school because it was too difficult, his decision was respected and appreciated. Fitzgerald and Goncu (in press) surmised that shared understanding will become possible only when home practices and knowledge are valued as highly as those of the school and its personnel. When Belenky et al. (1986) completed their research, they understood: "The stories of the women drew us back into a kind of knowing that had too often been silenced by the institutions in which we grew up and of which we were a part. In the end we found that, in our attempt to bring forward the ordinary voice, that voice had educated us" (p. 20). The families of our students had strong, individual voices, and did indeed educate us.

A word of encouragement

What advice can we offer you, the reader, for building home-school partnerships? You can reject the disabling myth that there is one right way for parents to become involved in their children's education. You can initiate a dialogue with colleagues and families about what they value, and then resist the urge to create a program. Instead, each teacher, with each family, could begin (and continue) developing forms of communication and building shared literacy opportunities. Will we do some of the same things in the same way next year? Maybe, maybe not. We've come to look forward to the developing instead of the implementing. But as we build on past experiences while negotiating a discourse with new voices, we'll be constantly looking at, and learning from, the next construction.

"School success is as much an act of social construction undertaken by families and schools as school failure has been shown to be," according to McLaughlin and Shields (1987, p. 158). Home-school partnerships can have a positive effect on literacy and learning for all parties if families and schools together develop ways of communicating, and build meaningful curriculum that extends the insular classroom community. The key elements of reciprocity and respect must be jointly constructed and locally interpreted. We offer our experiences as *one* such venture.

TWELVE
Questions and Answers and More Questions

Questions I have as a teacher

How do I prepare parents for journal writing?

Actually you don't; you prepare yourself. When Betty started the journals, she had no preconceived notion of what to expect. The use of the journal evolved into something different for each family. As whole language teachers, we appreciated and expected that our students would come to reading and writing in idiosyncratic ways. We were able to appreciate that families would become partners in their own unique ways. We have described our initial invitation to parents earlier in the book. In addition, we talked with parents at an open house early in the year.

Do you grade the students' journal writing?

No. The purpose of using the journals is to build bridges between home and school, not to evaluate the written responses that parents and children share in the journals.

What role did multicultural literature play in building literacy connections?

Several parents and children made strong connections to authors and events in books that were representative of their culture. Betty and Barbara made sure that their classroom libraries had a wide array of literature that included authors and illustrators from many cultures. African and African American authors were particularly emphasized, since the majority of our students were African American. We gave book talks, had author studies (e.g., Faith Ringold and Donald Crews), and often read these books aloud, all of which really stimulated student interest. When students chose books from the classroom library that they enjoyed, we helped them locate similar books in the school library.

What do I do when no one writes in the journal?

We simply wrote the date and "No Response." There was no scolding, no cajoling, just the simple statement of fact. It was successful with every family who did not initially respond (although most did respond at the first invitation in first grade, and all responded to the first invitation in second grade). The slowest engagement was five instances of "No Response" at the beginning of one journal in first grade, after which the family corresponded fairly faithfully for the rest of the year.

By second grade Barbara expected the children to respond even if a parent didn't have time to write. There were times when children reported that they hadn't had time, for one reason or another, and Barbara understood. However, when this seemed to be a pattern for a child who did not seem to be taking responsibility for his or her homework, Barbara handled it differently. She asked the child to tell her about the book; in most cases, the child had read the book. Then Barbara would say, "That's great—now go write what you just told me in your journal."

There are times in every family's life when there just isn't time to read or write, and we always empathized with the situation. We assured parents and children that the time together should be enjoyable and that we understood when circumstances intervened or when on occasion someone just plain didn't feel like responding.

Is it all right for a child not to respond independently in the journal?

It really depends on the purpose of the journal. If it is primarily for writing development, the student should be strongly encouraged to do the writing. If, as was the case for us, the primary purpose is for families to spend time together reading and talking about books, then who writes is not so important. It was important to us that each family find its own use for the journal, and it was not important that the uses be the same. However, there were times when we (or their parents) encouraged children to write some or all of the responses, when we thought it was time for a new kind of involvement.

What if a child chooses to copy text rather than write a response?

Among the journals we studied, there seemed to be a variety of reasons for copying text. Many of the children who began the year copying progressed to more independent responses in reply to teacher requests and questions. A few children stuck with this type of response all year, ignoring teacher requests and suggestions. The copying we observed took place in first grade; by second grade there were no children who chose to respond to their books by copying.

Kimberly copied parts of books throughout first grade. She used her journal to work through concepts about print. In this way, reading and writing remained obviously linked for Kimberly. Even when she began writing independent responses, she often copied part of the text first. At the beginning of the year she could not read what she wrote. At the end of first grade she could read some of what she wrote. Yet, by the end of second grade she was a capable reader, reading *PeeWee Scouts,* a short chapter book.

Kimberly's calendar was not the same as the school's calendar. She needed time, and she needed the respect of teachers who (while trying repeatedly throughout the year to expand this format) allowed her to move at her own pace, providing support for each tentative step. She found this so helpful that at the end of the year she said she would teach someone else to write the same way: "I look end [in] the book and I cary [copy] it in [and] wiriet it." By second grade she was no longer copying, although she often had someone at home help her with her responses.

What if children don't choose what we consider "good" literature?

We noticed that when children were beginning to read more independently, they enjoyed anything that they could read well. They often chose books that demonstrated their growing ability, with seeming disregard for story. It's like when a child first learns to ride a bike. It is a thrill just to ride, never mind where the bike is taking you. None of the children read this kind of book exclusively; there were too many other enticing choices.

What if the child is writing, but not about the books s/he reads?

We saw none of this in second grade and only a little of this type of unrelated response in first grade. Some children just seemed to have their own agenda for the journal and were not receptive to teachers' suggestions for change. This seems to be related to the time issue that the school imposes. By trusting the students and respecting their choices, we observed that the few children who clung to their own way of doing things eventually proved that they were taking a different road to becoming competent readers and writers.

Dumoneak used her journal as a practice book in first grade, a writing journal in which she included self-sponsored practice of familiar words and phrases, played with language, and eventually wrote lengthy stories. Betty tried intermittently to get at the books but was really very supportive of Dumoneak's choices. When Dumoneak was learning her address, she wrote, "Mrs.. Shockley I learn the address paper wood you mind if I write its!" Betty responded, "Not at all. You seem to be very good at deciding what kind of practice you need." However, a couple of entries later, when the writing seemed to have degenerated, Betty wrote, "I think you need to get a little more serious about your journal work now." When she didn't "get serious" in the next entry, Betty wrote, "What about the book you read?" Dumoneak dodged her with great skill, praising *Betty* as a good reader and writer. However, by the end of September of second grade, Dumoneak was writing three-page, detailed, interactive responses to books.

Will I always know the right thing to say for each child and each family?

No—at least we didn't. First, there is not one right thing to say, but an array of genuine responses. However, as researchers of the process, we did find that by studying our entries in relation to the family-child entry before and after, and by examining patterns across time, we got better at responding.

Will I always be able to engage both the child and the family?

We found this to be true in some cases, but not all. Sometimes we learned from talking with the children that although they did all the actual writing in the journal, their responses were supported by discussions with other family members. This was more common in second grade.

Is there a time for direct instruction in the journals?

We occasionally did provide very direct instruction, with great care that the conventions for writing never became the primary focus of the journals. Betty wrote to

Chris, "Let me teach you a new word—a b o u t." For the rest of the year Chris spelled *about* correctly. This was the only word Betty directly taught Chris through the journal. Most of the time Betty and Barbara simply modeled correct spellings, often consciously using in their own responses a word the child was misspelling. At times we asked a child to use a convention that we knew was understood, such as end punctuation or capitalization. These requests, two or three per year in most cases, were always made *after* we had responded to the content of the child's entry. In addition, many family members provided both reading and writing instruction.

What if parents are not comfortable with their own literacy?

Many parents who were not comfortable with their own literacy found a way to respond in the journals. One parent drew pictures that illustrated her son's and her responses to the books. Another parent copied text from the book lightly, or with dots, and had her son trace over the letters. Betty responded by writing, "You and your mama are good writers," and later in the year, "Andrew tells me how hard you both work with the books at night. Your writing is beautiful. Thank you." Some parents apologized for their spelling or handwriting. Yet their desire to help their child overcame their reluctance to expose any lack of writing skills they felt they had.

What about families who don't speak English?

You can encourage them to listen to their child read or to tell stories from pictures. You might suggest involving other family members or friends.

Pakaysanh's family spoke their native language; English was a second language. Early in the year his father and other family members copied parts of the text into the journal. They continued this support until Pakaysanh could read and respond to Betty's questions on his own. Later, Pakaysanh did almost all the writing. However, he reported in his journal that he often read the books to his parents.

How can I respond when a child writes using letter strings or other preconventional forms?

Marianesha wrote page after page of letter strings in first grade. Betty's first response was simply, "I love you." She then began to encourage family participation: "Could someone write and tell me about Marianesha's reading times?" After several such entries, with no responses, Betty again addressed Marianesha, asking her to leave spaces between her words so Betty could read her writing. After several requests, Marianesha copied a list of spelling words. On January 12, Betty wrote, "Let's see if you can write—I love you!" Marianesha copied every word of Betty's entry. They followed this pattern for a while. Suddenly, in February, Marianesha began writing variations of a phrase ("I Love Mom I Mom Love . . ."). She continued this pattern, expanding with additional words, through the end of the year. In daily writing workshop her writing began to look more like the other children's, with spacing and page layout, even though she continued prephonemic writing.

Questions I have as a parent

All this sounds like fun, but will it help my child become a better reader or writer?

The children began first grade with a range of understanding about reading. There were children with very little letter-sound awareness and children with great understanding, ready to take the steps to become independent readers. Even though some children were not independent readers at the beginning of second grade, by the end of the year every child scored either "adequate" or "excellent" on the second-grade Houghton Mifflin Periodic Reading Survey. Not one student scored in the "needs improvement" range.

Both teachers and parents felt that the journals were instrumental in helping these young literacy learners. Colin's mother wrote to Betty at the end of first grade:

> Reading through his journal tonight I can see how far he's come with writing his thoughts about the stories he's read . . . something which once almost intimidated him has become a pleasurable activity.

At the end of second grade she wrote the following to Barbara in response to a questionnaire:

> Colin has spent his first two weeks of summer vacation in several quiet (and therefore surprising) ways—reading the sports section of the *Atlanta Constitution*, perusing sports and comic books, drawing and writing. He can't help but continue "Reading Workshop" and "Writing Workshop" on his own—it has become such a large part of his life.

The growth parents and teachers saw was as individual as the children who did the growing. We saw Chris grow from a struggling first grader to an independent reader of chapter books. We saw Colin begin to extend his notions of his "good books." We saw many children expand their reading strategies as they branched out into new genres and lengthier reading materials.

My son does his reading very well for me, but getting him to write is another story! What should I do?

Adam's mom wrote this question to Betty in first grade. Betty responded:

> Adam has made so much progress in reading—doing it in his own time. I suspect writing will become more comfortable for him with time too. Adam seems to like to play it safe, and then when he's mastered something, he wows you. I think he's telling us to trust him on this writing thing. I'd just continue with what's working for him.

How long should I continue to write my child's responses?

Let the child take the lead. Sometimes the teacher suggested that the child take over part of the writing. Many children in the beginning would alternate, with parents writing sometimes, children writing at others. Sometimes the child, although capable, would be too tired to write. We never intended this homework to take all evening.

It seemed to be important to both parents and children that parents maintained some kind of role. For some, it was reading the book together, with the child writing the response. For others, it was the child's reading the book and the two talking about it. Cathy wrote about this role reversal (and the realities of fatigue) in her journal: "I've been reading it to my mom and she's been falling asleep."

Parents often have a feel for what will be most helpful for their child. For example, at the beginning of the year, Brad's mom recorded Brad's response; later, he wrote his own responses, and his mom added hers. She maintained a role but did not keep a role Brad no longer needed her to take.

What if my child is not enjoying reading time?

Often when parents shared their child's frustration about shared reading, we found that it had become a tense time in which the child was worried about not being able to meet the parent's expectations. Several times Barbara and Betty reminded parents who were worried about the child's performance that it was the enjoyment of the book and the time together that were most important. They also tried to reassure the parents about their child's progress. Sometimes parents had to reassure themselves, as when LaToya's mom wrote:

> LaToya enjoys reading time. She always reminds me that she has a book to read. Sometimes she gets a little upset when she can't remember the words or if she don't know a word. And sometimes I get upset if she don't remember; but we always pull ourselves together and keep trying.

How might reading and writing together at home affect my child's attitudes about reading?

The parents we spoke with felt that their children had a very positive attitude toward reading. Cathy's mom said, "It made us both aware of authors. I think that will help her when she's older." In first grade Adam's mom wrote, "We have lots of fun. Thank you for the books!" Adrian's mom felt that "having the journal made him more intent in his reading." At the end of second grade LaToya's mom wrote:

> LaToya has come along way this year. She trys to read anything and everything. Every night when it's time to read her book; she will come to me and say "Mom you know reading is important." LaToya loves to read now. She seems to want time alone so she can have her own space and she will sit back and read.

In an end-of-year survey almost every parent reported that their child "loved reading" or "liked to read very much."

We have lots of extended discussions about books, but my child only writes down a few sentences. What should I do?

You are doing it. Reading and talking about books is really the most important thing.

When my child can read independently, should I still read to her?

Yes. Even when children have the ability, they sometimes do not have the stamina to read longer books. For example, Cathy wanted her mom to read *The Boxcar Children*. It was during the World Series, and the family cheered on the home team Braves, but her mom found time to read aloud during the commercials. Even when children can read fluently, there is just something special about being read to. It is a unique way of experiencing something together, with discussions taking place during instead of after reading. In addition, parents can introduce children to books they might not pick up on their own, as Colin's mom did when he refused to try anything beyond his favorite authors and genres.

My child is doing well with his writing, but he seems to have a problem sounding words out in his reading. How should I help him?

When a parent asked Barbara this question in the journal, Barbara responded:

> Chris is doing much better with his writing. He's making a lot of effort and you can see the results of it. His writing will help him with remembering the sounds letters make. Some words are hard to sound out. You might ask him, "What would make sense here?" Then he can see if the word he couldn't read has the right letter sounds. Also many times skipping a word he doesn't know and reading to the end of the sentence can help him figure the word out. When he's struggling to sound out a word and not having success, encourage him to try one of these other strategies. Ms. M.

I think my child should finish the books he brings home every night. He is bringing home longer books that he doesn't have time to finish. Could you be sure he brings home books that he can finish?

This question came from Chris' family and helped Barbara realize a misunderstanding about the homework assignment. Chris was a "closet chapter book reader" at school but would never take them home because of this misunderstanding. So Barbara wrote:

> To Mom & Dad—Chris is starting to read longer books. I know you're proud of him, I am! He may want to read part of the same book each night and use a book marker to keep his place. He read me a chapter book this week—just one chapter a day. He could do the same for his homework.

My child has become a very independent reader. He wants to do all the writing in his journal. What can I do to stay involved with his reading?

As the children began to read longer books and become more competent readers, their parents' role in their literary lives changed. This was a difficult transition for many parents, and they felt at a loss as to what they should do to continue their relationship around books.

You might read the same book as the child, then discuss it. You also might try reading an adult book in the same genre as the book the child is reading, then discuss similarities and differences, likes and dislikes. When Colin was reading versions of

Sherlock Holmes stories written for children, his mother checked out the original Sherlock Holmes from the library. She read some of the stories aloud to Colin.

As teacher-researchers, we still have questions

Now that we have studied the process for two years, what will we do differently next year?

We asked parents to "tell me about your child" at the beginning of the year. Next time, we'll follow that by telling families about ourselves, our own children, our teaching, and ourselves as readers and writers.

We would continue this more personal connection throughout the year by sharing more of the books we are reading with parents and encouraging them to share their reading with us. We did this sporadically, as opportunities presented themselves in the journals. We also brought books to, or talked about books, at most of our parent meetings. But we'd like to do more.

Do some children and parents need more examples of ways to respond to books?

In analyzing the journal interactions over time, we wondered if we should have been more explicit sometimes and more open-ended at others. When some children and parents did not respond to suggestions, we wondered if we should have provided more models.

We often saw an over-reliance among family members on sounding out unknown words. We suggested that parents use alternative strategies such as making a guess, checking picture clues, and reading to the end of the sentence. We also pointed out that some words just aren't spelled the way they sound. Next time we'd offer specific examples to illustrate our point.

We have many more questions. Will children or families become tired of the journals if they are used year after year? What would happen if children wrote to each other, as Nancie Atwell's eighth graders did? Are there other ways of connecting with families as students grow older? The joy of being researchers is that we can begin today investigating these questions, and posing new ones. Won't you join us?

APPENDIX A
Dennis' Family Reading Journal

" The Gunnywolf " **DENNIS**

Ms. Shockley:

I was thinking maybe the book was to hard for Dennis, he tells me he wanted to read himself than he told me to read it to him. he learned a lot of words one what I did't know when he does! we went through the story together laughing and reading. It was real fun. I enjoyed it and he enjoyed it too. he is really learning to read well and I'm proud of him.

Dennis Sims
(mother)

I'm really proud of him too. He really loves that book. After I read it to the class

---

the first time, Dennis carried it around with him most of the day. He always asks for it at reading time. Thank you so much for writing to me in the journal. It means a lot to me and to Dennis. He's a great guy and you must be a great ...!

Mom!

"The Gunnywolf" again ←I told you!!! He loves that book!

Dennis wanted no help at all (he said).

mamma I want to read it by myself.

and he did just that & only had to tell him about 2 @ 3 words. Then later on that night he reread it again to his Dad. that's one book that gets him real excited.

So I won't be surprised if he picks it out to bring home again; his beginning to see he having fun while doing it. That's the whole idea here — to "learn good" and have fun while doing it."

He can take that book home as often as it's available (sometimes others might beat him to it!) You can order him

---

"Where is everybody"

He wanted to read the animals names himself and wanted me to read where each one was.

Dennis response:
{I liked. The Lion, and the bee}

His trying to write he liked the lions and the dogs, he said that on (Dog that's a cursive g).

This is it! I love the way you are sharing with each other and sharing with me. I look forward to a wonderful year together.

I liked your lion Dennis! I wish you could see my cat. She looks like a little tiger. Do you have any pets? We have goldfish.

Freight Train

We read together and when we got to the train with the colors, Dennis named all the colors. and as I was reading he was making noise like a train. cho-choo, he said that's the way he and the other students were doing while you were reading the story. If you try...

his own copy by calling Amy book store in Athens — That would be a great surprise. Thanks again for writing to me.

(He wanted to draw a lion and self that...
(He wanted to tell you how he sees my cat)

Lion

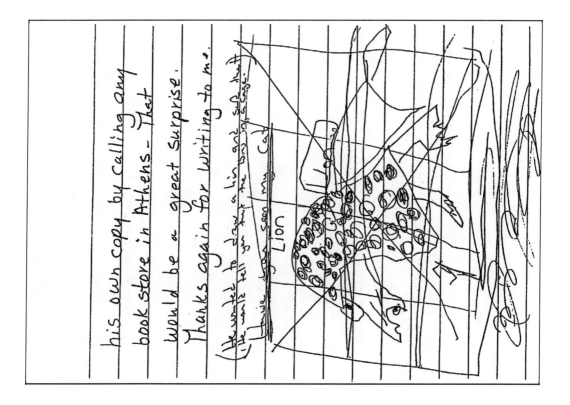

10-1-92

I'm so glad Dennis got to sort of relive the class experience with this book by sharing it with you. It does make the book better when you add the sound effects. The children thought of doing it - not me. It was fun.

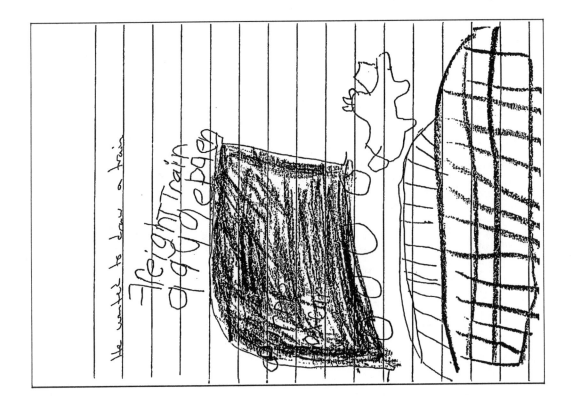

He wanted to draw a train

Freight Train

10-6-92

I'm so glad you enjoyed the book and your time together. Thanks for writing me the note about Dennis' finger too. When it happened I sent him to the office to be checked and to get some ice for the swelling (He said he forgot to tell you that)

(10-7-92) "Bells"

Dennis reads well in this book by himself his Dad was really amazed and we replied where did Little Dennis learn to read like this?

10-2-92 No Response ("Sorry" but have taken stron since reading that made me sleep all night (10-5-92) I certainly understand - I hope you're feeling better Here are my thoughts

we really had a fun time, we read the story 3 Times, the first time I helped him with some words, the second time he did much better, but the third time he did it all by himself, he was great. I didn't have to tell him one word. I gave him a big hug and told him he did a great job.

exactor
seeing
and
crying

Boy
BABIES

told him that you be going and the books in the classroom too with all the kids at school this really is a good thing that youre doing together. It lets us know really how well hes doing at school by telling me how the baby that he was in class in the classroom at home with us. Dennis has no response his time. I guess his tired because he read a lot and its late too.

I bet he was tired — that's a lot of reading. I appreciate a lot of reading. I appreciate so much all you share with me about how you and Dennis and his father are feeling about school and Dennis' interests and progress.

I am very excited to get to know you all this year.

(10-8-92)

"Truck"

He is involved a few weeks on his own. One was producing what he sows. Lot in the bible. Its really not much we talked about it except the way a truck takes lots of things places and how it stops for gas and drives in bad weather and lots of traffic and following Directions.

10-9-92 It sounds like you did quite a lot with a book

The Gunnywolf.
he read most of the book to
me, but I helped him A little bit.

Dennis.

(Dennis said his dad
wrote this)

1-5-93
So - the Gunnywolf
goes to Dennis' house
again! You know he told
us it was his favorite
book way back at the
beginning of the year.
He told me this morning
though that he could now
read the whole book by
himself. He was very proud.

that didn't have many words
in it. That is just the kind
of sharing time I'd hoped
everyone could have. Thank
you.

(10-12-93)
" The Gunnybread Boy"
He wanted to draw a
going from the book.
Great!

10-13-92

Dennis was so excited to find this book in our library. We had to read it once right then and there —

He joined right in with my reading. He's learning fast.

(10-14-92)

The Gunnywolf

He read the story almost by himself. I see what you mean when you ●. So he could take the book home as much as he likes; the more he brings it, the better he reads it. he loves a lot of the words on his own. The more he brings it home, the better he

gets. he's doing great, and what makes I wonderful his always willing to learn.

Isn't it fun to watch? Kids are amazing — especially Dennis. I think he knows what he likes and how to learn from what he reads. With your support and positive attitude combined with Dennis, I'm very excited about the possibilities for Dennis. Thanks so much for your time.

(10-15-92)(I'm Bigger than you)

He was so anxious to read it to me, he rushed me out the shower. I only had to tell him one or 2 words, he did great.

(It's a Perfect Day)

I was thinking maybe this was a little bit hard for Dennis, then I saw the big words, but he surprised me. He liked all the different sounds the animals made, he knew mostly all of them he had fun laughing and reading.

10-16-92 Dennis was still excited this morning. He announced he could read

I'm Bigger Than You to the whole class.

I thought it was neat that Dennis wanted to take 2 books home last night too.

(10-19-92) Dan on Scary House

Dennis did o.k. reading the story I helped him with a few words, and I asked his opinion of the books. and he wanted to do a scary house.

10-21-92

It will be interesting again to see how he does with that book the next time he brings it home.

He was one of the characters in the book Hattie and the Fox that we performed today. I bet you enjoy this book tonight.

(Hattie and the Fox)

I had to clap my hands to his reading this book. I was really amazed at how well he did. He read the words so smoothly and clearly. It was fun. (over!)

(Space race)

Dennis liked it ok. but he said he liked Hattie and the Fox better. In space race he couldn't read a lot of the words. So I read it and let him said the count down from 10 to zero, and everytime a ship was out of the way I would ask him how many left and so on. It was fun but not so exciting.

10-22-92

I knew you guys would have fun with Hattie and the Fox and I agree that Space Race just doesn't measure up. Sounds like you made the best of it though by using

(Anansi and the moss-covered Rock)
to be honest, when I looked at this
book I said to myself, what a long hard
maybe boring book, but I was really wrong...
and surprised I enjoyed it. it was terrific
and fun. Dennis knew some words. He kept
looking through the pages saying how many
left to read. He was getting impatient. So I
told him I'll read the rest of it so I let him
read when enthusiasm fell down KPOM. He
liked that so we ended up making it fun. That's
a real good book.

10-23-92
Dennis Started to take
The _Gunniwolf_ home again

---

the counting sequence to
put a little life into things.
Your reading new books to
Dennis is just as helpful
as Dennis reading familiar
books to you. Kind of like
sharing the joy.

Dennis just told me he
read the books to his
— Hattie and the Fox
dad this morning too.
That is so great.
He said you were both
proud of him and he was
proud of himself too.

woke up will about 5:00 this morning. I tell him to wait until time for him to get up at 6:30. Then he hurried to get to he really enjoyed it with the flip up pages. He wanted to know what he liked.

but then he stopped and said "I think I'll take my other favorite book home" and he gathered up Anansi And The Moss Covered Rock. We did a play of this story at school too. I'm glad you liked the book too. You and Dennis must have similar preferences.

(Answers @ the pen pal kids.)
He and his dad read this book.
He couldn't read it last night because he went to sleep early and didn't

10-27-92

That is amazing.
Isn't it exciting being
with a child so eager
to learn. Bless you all!

Dennis, I love your
drawings!

(10-29-92) Teeny Tiny
We read this book together. He knew
some and I read the other. It was fun
He said the most exciting lines and did
in the way it was suppost to be said. when
the voice got louder and louder and lady end

when the tiny woman responded back.
Tales 2. that was exciting.
...he wanted to ghost. like in the
book So! Halloween.

11-10-92
When I read
your responses,
it makes me
wish we had
a video camera
recording your
time together.
It sounds so
wonderful. Bless
you both.

He did a great job.
He gave himself a
star

(On A Hunt we will go)

H F I DID iT ALL BY MY SELF
cLoSeD MY
eyes too. and I
Did IT riGht.
WiThOUT MY MOM
HeLp

I really didn't have to help him at all,

He read it by himself.

11-12-92

I love this shared writing
I think you both have very
nice handwriting. Dennis
read to me today and at
times covered his eyes to

show me how well he
remembered the story
He has good reason to be
very proud of himself.

(Madeline)

Dennis started out reading with a little
help from me. then I could see him getting
impatient from all the other pages? so I
him till read some and he listen so he said
ok. but he never stopped reading he told to
read along with me. I didn't mention it to
him I just kept on reading. and he was reading
along with me. Some words I knew that he
knew did stop but I'll make out so so we

BIG — ReD — BARN.

REMEMBER
The LITTLE
PuPPy-DoGS,
aNd-The-Big-Cow,
aNd-The-FiELD
Mouse in the corn.
Field.

Corn
Dog
Laughing
Mouse
Laughing

---

made a sort long book for us. we read it together.

11-16-92

Your sensitivity and understanding of Dennis' needs as a young reader are just the ticket to helping him continue to believe in his own abilities and stay motivated. I'm very impressed by your relationship. Thank you again for sharing such special times with me.

I Did all

4   Books

① The cow That Oink Oink

② Our Granny

③ Snakes

④ Bussing Flies

11-19-92

Dennis that is really nice.
I'm so glad you like to
read. I love to read too.
Which book was your
favorite?

11-17-92

WOW Dennis! Way to
go! That was wonderful
hot shot! You are just
getting smarter and
smarter!

silly things." (God) whatever bay and cause are they.

Dennis, he knows what he has to do and he tries his best to do it. In certain parts he tells me ("don't help me with this memory) I can read it by myself. his so willing to learn.

Hold Your Nose here

comescloos

Skunk

I did 3 Books and Mom Helps Me WITh SPaCe RaCe

1-20-92

No wonder you've turned into such a good reader and writer.

Thanks mom for the help. I can tell it's important to Dennis.

You both deserve the award for "Best Effort" that Dennis will receive next week.

I Like Stop and go. I Like the color The yollow Buses. and see you later. and I Like coming Home. and I Like school I hate when school over. and I Like school go every moreck stop stop

Dennis

12-3-92
I think it's time for a new journal!
I was so glad to know that Dennis is feeling so good about himself as a reader and writer.
Believing in yourself is so important and you seem to know just how to help him feel that way.

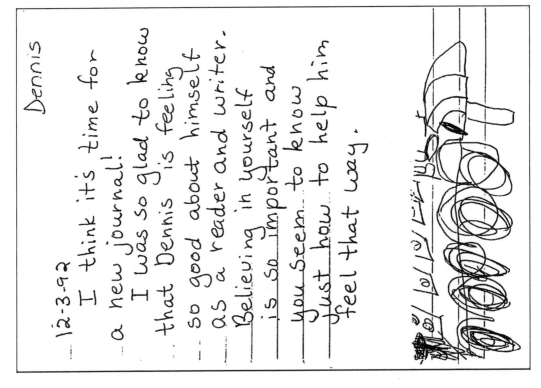

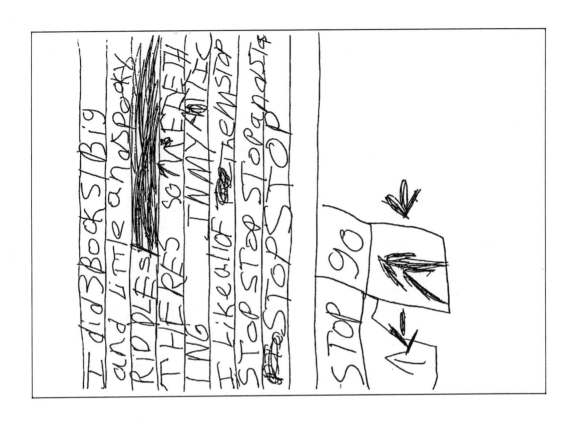

12-7-92

I really liked the book. you made at home over the weekend. You are growing up and learning fast.

Animalia (and) Big Pumpkin I read both books to dennis because they were sorta hard. Animalia was not too exciting Dennis almost went to sleep all he had to say is mom the words rhyme don't they.
but when i started to reading Big Pumpkin he got all into it. I read a page then ask him about what happen to see how well he will listen and understand. he knew everything I ask him we had fun with that book. I can tell he enjoyed it a lot.

Father Christmas
I WAS GETTING for christmas Legos, bicycle, and A batman tape. and A binbag and A lot of clothes.
I like santa claus and their rein deers.
I like to see santa claus going down the chimney. and one more thing,
I like when santa claus get back home, 12-10-92 so he can be warm. That is so nice of you to think about Santa Claus' feelings. you might even get an extra present for that nice thought.
The End
I LOVE BOOK

① Theres something in my attic
② Pretend youre a cat.

Well Dennis told me to write something, I could tell he was tried and sleepy but he did well he helped with pretend your a cat..

I'm very proud of him too. Thanks for your time and support

Dennis

(Let's Jump)

Noone jumped out
We can jump

here all
Morning. 74
We can jump 51
all day

We all
(Where's God Going)

Dennis wanted me to write about God. He didn't know some words so he told me to read most of it. It's a good book. (cont)

But on the book. Let's Jump. he said mama I want to write about it myself. So I sit ok. and he said, is he writes a lot that his teacher will be proud of him. he actually wanted to fill the whole page up and then some on the other page. I told him that's enough, I may not be writing on the lines, because their so hard to see in his tablet. he really is doing well. you're right!

1-7-93
I tell you what- that
Dennis is one great guy.
Isn't it wonderful to
see him so eager to
take on a challenge
like reading harder books
and trying to write a
whole page. He's right-

Dennis is having such a positive experience with you and his books. I hope Dennis always feels this way about books and that he always takes his responsibilities so seriously.

Heckedy Peg

As soon as I picked Dennis up from the Daycare he told me "momma I have a great book, and I want you to read it for me when we get home." he kept saying it over and over again every once in a while. until I finally read it. I have to admit it + was a ▓ wonderful book. I'd read a little then ask him questions about what had just happened, to see how well he was listening.

I am very proud of him..

Big and Little

He did just great. the only 2 words I had to tell him was Cubs and children. he always is so anxious when he brings books home, he says don't forget, I have to read my books.

Pitch your ball spot!

again he surprised me by reading some of the bigger words like Didn't, Swallow, Sandy. Dennis says he loves the pp up pages. he loves to read.

1-11-93

I am always so eager to read your responses because I know

days of the week.

"Chicken Soup with Rice"
Dennis told me what to write he
said. I read chicken soup with me,
and I read it by my self with a
little b.t of help from my momma.
Was right he did great. again I was
amazed by all the words he knew on
his own. and he said his teacher will
be proud of him.

"Hecledy Peg"
Dennis said I liked the book and I get
sleepy when my mom had to stop reading and
talk on the phone. I think that Dennis
wants me to keep reading until he can learn
to read it himself. we again had fun.
The End

---

he answered everything right and I
even let him read some, everything they
had the children's names monday, Tuesday,
wednesday thursday friday, saturday and sunday
I'd stop and let him read their names
than I'd continue reading the story. we
had fun. It's really a great book. Dennis
says so too.

1-12-93
I am so glad to know you
both found a new book to
love. Like The Gunniwolf
book. Dennis tells me he's
going to check out
Hetkeety Peg again. That
was such a neat way to
let Dennis share in the
reading of a book he loves
- letting him read the names-

He did great on the Gunnywolf, I had to help him a little bit with some words. But he told me to read Heckedy Peg and let him read the children names at one point. I told me to let him read on his own, he read one or two lines, then he told me to go ahead and finish, he'll learn how to read it one day because you can but hell keep on bugging at home.

Yes! We certainly can see how Dennis likes to teach himself how to read. You are both super special. Dennis is learning so much! BY Mary Hall!!

I did small us a cricket BY YW SELF.

(next page)

1-14-93
I think you are so right about Dennis' plan to learn to read the book Heckedy Peg by first listening to you read it over and over. You have been your child's best teacher. Could you write a book about it yourself sometime?

I will Peg to Heckedy BY Dennis
PEG all the time
To Be Learning

The End

1-22-93

Dennis you told me I
was going to be proud
of you when you
first entered the room
this morning - And you
know what- I really
am. I really liked
it when you told the
Gunnywolf story this
morning too.

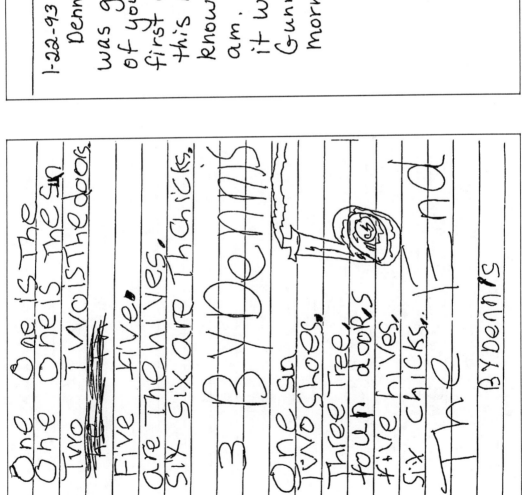

One One is the sun
One One is the sun
Two Two is the doors.

Five Five
are the hives,
Six Six are the chicks,

3 BYDeNNS

One sun
Two shoes
Three tree
four doors
five hives,
Six chicks.
The end
BYDennis

2-1-93   So what . . . . . ?
Did you get to finish
your writing.? I bet
you could read that book
all by yourself. Did
your family like it too.?

BY Dennis andDennis
I Like The fat Pig
I LiKe The hot IAGS
I LiKe COLD LittLe PiGS
I LiKe CLean LittLe PiGS
I LiKe gooD LittLe PiGS
and OneMore So...

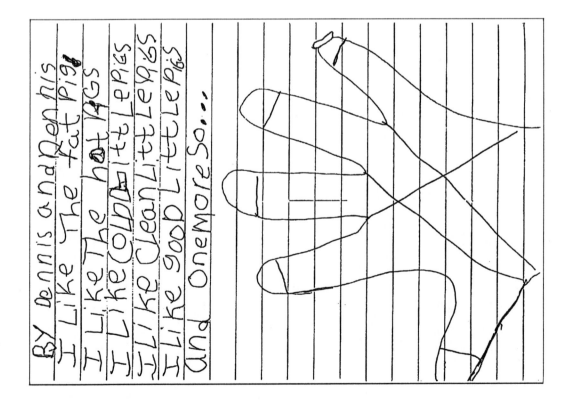

By Dennis

COOKIES WEEK

On Monday she Was Being Bad and fell in the toilet But she knocked The Plant Down The Windowsill The End

BI Bt

2-3-93

Pumpkin Cat almost fell in the toilet yesterday!

I really love your writing Dennis! You have learned so much so fast.

---

① Books ② and Little. ③ I love my Family. ④ Bread, ⑤ Shapes, Little Sister

Dennis was very great with his reading. I only had to tell him a few words. I have a feeling he's gonna be an A student like his little sister. She's real smart too.

2-4-93

I have the same feeling. Dennis is doing great and best of all he loves to learn and challenges himself to get better and better. Your family obviously plays a big part in this wonderful attitude.

going to read them all.
He is writing a really
great book at school
too. It's Called - My School
It is really good.
By dennis

The Better
To Eat yo u my Dear
Cried The WoLf
The End The End
Red
RiD ing
FlooD

---

⑤ books again ① Houses God Say you
② I can fly ③ Down to town ⑤ coloreey
week. I asked Dennis why do
he bring so many books home he said
"momma I want to learn a lot." I
colliit or gave with that is on one book
Colires week. he tried to Shaw how small
he was by reading whats on the next
page before he turns the page. he was
trying to show off in front of his Soot
cousin Iron othth

2-8-93
That Dennis is one
special kid! when I
Saw Dennis with 5 books
again I wondered too
but he said he was

2-10-93

"Ms. Shockley, Ms. Shockley
what big arms you have!"
"The better to give you
a great big hug my dear!"

A big hug for doing such
good work!

"Little Red Riding Hood"
I'll write since dennis was so busy with
his valentine cards. Big Dennis and Little
Dennis were reading together. Dennis was
reading the notes he knows. he is so
determined to read that book. He sure is
trying hard.

2-15-93 You are so right.
He is writing great stories too.

"It's a Perfect Day."
We made up a song about
Old McDonald had
a farm with the animals
in the Book! It was
fun. (WiTha E I E I O.)
The-End

... we went over the spelling words for
Friday test. He did great. He spelled all
of them. He only had trouble with one
"Shll." I'm so proud of him. His smart!

2-16-93

Every time I read a new
book to the class Dennis
is the first one to ask
to take that book home!

By Dennis (Lonbro)

I Like When
They Pull The
Basket up and
Dawn They Let go and
you go

The End

They
End

By Dennis Morris Themos Morris
I Read The Morris

The moose=o
When Morris
Said You are a
Moose Said Morris

By Dennis ⊗ You are a
Deer I Like
When The Deer
Said you are
a Deer Said
Ginedeer youis
a Deer you are
a Deer I Like
When The cow
Said Las. oK Some
Body else
um The page

(The Napping House) 2-22-93

Dennis again Dr. great he shirked off reading in a singing voice. It was sometimes when he was reading this story when it got difficult and he had to keep reading the lines one over and over I had to tell me to help but when he got near the end of the book he would slow down and start lines but then he turned the page he was showing off. he well he remember he had. Dennis is a fun guy as well as being a super reader. "Somebody and the three Bears" Dennis wanted me to read it for him but he followed along as I traced the words. he also was asking me where each word was when I'd stop the story.   It is. I wish I'd had the idea first and written that book.

Dennis said
I Like The Book
Read The Hole Book
By my SeLf
I Like The White
Pig The End

1-1 Read 4 Books
By my self
1-1 Read Painting??
and Baby Gets Dressed
and I love My Family
and Stripes.

2-24-93
Way to go Dennis! I really loved the way you told the story of Somebody and the Three Blairs too.

"The Gunnywolf"
We Like This Book Better Than The Other Gunnywolf I Like Kum~

Kwakhi illa kumkwa
Whi, illa
"Flying"

Flying is The Best Book

3-1-93
Why did you like this version best? I remember Dennis saying the other Gunniwolf was his favorite book in the whole world. Isn't it interesting how our ideas can change with time.

3-4-93

Dennis you did a great job writing and reading your own Three Billy Goats Gruff book in School. You are amazing! LOVED This Book

My Mom Dad

HaLep Me Bec.s

I LiVed

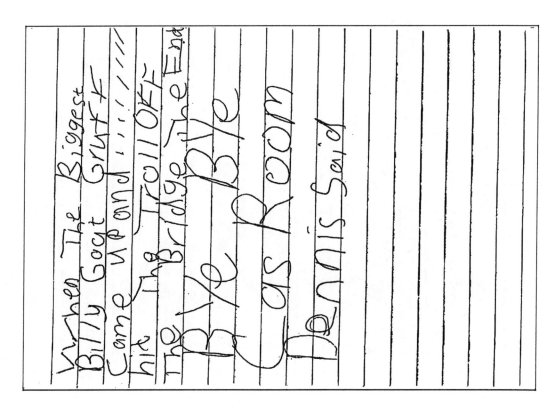

"The Book"

Mrs Shelby, Dans is trying to learn to spell words on his own... what slows down his progress is the way he can...

All Shelby yp

When The Biggest Billy Goat Gruff came up and !!!! /////
hit the Troll OFF The Bridge The End

Bye Bye Bye as Room

Dennis said

3-11-93

You are nice too Dennis
and I'm so happy you
like to read and write.
Do you ever make up
stories and tell them
to your friends or
family? Yes

For Dennis Friend (3-11-93)
I Loved The Book
It was nice So ve
Dice nice #1
he yellow map
It is my Book.
you Not I Like it
The END

(3-18-93)
Three up a tree
Dennis
The Ball is a scary
Cat and the Chicken
is too you are nice
Ms. Shockly
Thelma

3-31-93

Dennis I'm so happy that you like books so much. I think you are a really really great guy too!

4-1-93

Dennis It's been having a rough time this week he's not get back into his reading at home yet. I think it's because of the spring break last week. we shuttle reading the book last night but Dennis was asleep before we finished I think he's got to get back into it.

Dennis says [2-94]

Book I Like The book was so nice and it was so so good Really Really good good guy and you are Nice you are The Best teacher and mrs. I love(n) teend

Books, as I was reading he was following along. At some point I would stop and try to get him to read a little but he would tell me to go ahead he would me to read it to him, so I DR.

At very fun.

4-19-93

That sounds just wonderful to me. Even though Dennis is a good reader now, there's no substitute for being read ~~to~~ to sometimes

---

4-13

I Read
a Books
They Are...
Spring and
The Story

4-13-93

I think you mean that you read 2 stories in 1 book. I'm glad you like the Frog and Toad stories, I do too.

4-13-93

"Rumpelstiltskin"
Dennis said he couldn't think of anything. So we both enjoyed the

4-21-93 No Response "Sorry."
We had read 1 @ 2 chapters in
The Gray book. but it [illegible] my
mind about the journal.

4-22-93.
The lense-High men (out of Aku Tales)
I asked Dennis which story he was
suppose to read. and he said, let me
show you the "contents". Then he said Mrs.
Shockley said to practice "The Fance and
the Snake. So we read it. He knows a
lot of the words himself. I only helped
him when a few. He DR Great.

(4-23-93)
The Gungwolf
I think that maybe he keeps the
other Gungwolf books the shirt Seem

---

really interested, we read the whole together.
We read some, I read some, and so on.

5-1-93
You guys continue to do
such wonderful things
with books. I'm so glad
Dennis knows he can do
things like practice a
story until he knows it
well enough to tell it
and/or read it to others.
I'm also glad he knows
that some books and
stories are better than
others. Great job!
(5-3-93)
"Somebody" and The Three Bears

permission to Copy it
and use it in a book
I want to write this
summer about the
wonderful things
parents do with their
children to support
reading and writing.
I think you and Dennis
are geniuses!

(5-5-93)

Denny and Madge (spelling Denny in the)
Dennis read the first story again he
showed me the content and The first
story which he needs to tell him
Even weeks and I coll see he was
getting bored and sleepy. So I asked

Dennis read really good I only told him
about 4 @ 5 words when he finished reading
I clapped my hands and gave him a big
hug on the cheek and told him he did great.
his really becoming a smart child. I was
just thinking to myself, its a child has a
wonderful teacher and wonderful parents that
takes up time with him and help him to
read and learn new things he has out to
be a genius. what I think my little Denny
will be someday.

5-5-93
Your writing gave me
chill bumps! I am so
impressed by this idea
of yours. I would like
very much to have your

him. I he would like me to read the next story, Christmas Eve Dinner. he said yes. So when I finished he said momma go ahead and read the last one so I said o.k. and he went to sleep time the story was over about (8:15 pm)..

5-6-93
You know, one of the things I admire so much about you as Dennis' teacher and mom, is that you're always so sensitive to his needs and feelings. I bet Dennis felt so special again last night. What a wonderful way

to go to sleep!

I would still like to have your permission to share your writing ~~~ You have my permission to do whatever you like. Thanks so much! You are very special.
Days with Frog and Toad (5-10-93)

I read One Book Because my Mom Said read how Many I Can My Day read With Me the End

5-12-93 That's wonderful Dennis! You are a very

Smart young man.
I have loved being
friends with you and
your family this year.
I'll miss reading your
journal every morning
I wish you all the
very, very best!

(5-13-93)
Teeny Tiny

Dennis read this book just great. I
told him only 2 words I overlooked
① which. He read this book the way
It was supposed to be read when the
voice was teeny tiny he read it soft
"Give me my bone" But when the voice got loud
he read it a little loud. "GIVE ME my

Cont.
BONE". And the last time much
lol. Then when the teeny tiny woman
answered he was so excited he
TAKE IT! I was excited to
I had forgotten how the story ends. I
was so proud of him I clapped my hands,
and told him he read the story just perfect.
He's really learned a lot this year.
Thank you for being such a wonderful
teacher. Dennis told me he likes you
a lot.

APPENDIX B

Research Processes for *Engaging Families* (or, What We Did on Our Summer Vacations)

Developing the questions

Our research questions, which evolved continually, included the following:

Primary questions

- How can elementary teachers affect the family-school literacy relationship?
- How is the child's literacy learning affected if the family-school literacy relationship is strengthened?
- What family literacy events can teachers learn about that will help them support school literacy learning?
- What school literacy events can families learn about that will help them support home literacy learning?

Secondary questions

- What forms and forums will families create, given the opportunity to share time with their children focused on books and to correspond with the teacher about the process?
- How can teachers, children, and parents better understand the various cultures represented in their extended community through shared reading and writing experiences?
- What relationships will be formed over two years among teachers, parents, and children through the home-school reading journals?
- How will parents, teachers, and children develop as readers, responders, writers, and correspondents?
- What are teachers, parents, and children learning, with two years of similar instruction and home-school connections?
- What similarities and differences are there for second graders compared with first graders?

- What similarities and differences are there for two different groups of first graders?
- Will these "two-year" parents and children continue to have an active voice in the school lives of the children? Have they been empowered?

Gathering information

Figure B-1 shows the year we began with Lakendra, Adrian, and Cathy's class, their movement to second grade, and the adoption of the parallel practices in various teaching settings.

As a teacher-researcher, Betty has for years viewed her classroom as "data world," a place where remarkable things happen every day for her to gather, ponder, and interpret in relation to future teaching decisions. Consequently, she collected a great deal of information and asked parental permission to share with others what they were learning together, even though the first year was not designed as a research study. During the second year of the study we were systematic in our data collection of the same sources of information and some additional ones (see Figure B-2).

	1991–1992	*1992–1993*	*1993–1994*
Betty	Established parallel practices, original twenty families	New group of twenty first-grade families	Sabbatical at University of Georgia, Athens
Barbara		Adapted parallel practices with original twenty families, now in second grade	Moved to new school; adapted practices with families of new third graders
JoBeth			Incorporated parallel practices in teacher education courses

FIG. B-1.   *Implementation of Parallel Practices*

Information Source	*When Collected*
Tell me about your child	Beginning of each year
Home interest inventory	First grade: beginning of year
Clay's word-writing task	First grade: beginning, middle, end of year
Standard topic writing	First, second grades: beginning, middle, end of year
Informal reading inventory	First, second grades: beginning, middle, end of year
Samples of daily writing	First, second grades: various times
Houghton Mifflin periodic reading survey	Second grade: quarterly
Home-school reader response journals	First, second grades: all year
Family stories	First, second grades: various times
Parent reflections and expectations survey	First, second grades: end of year
Student reflections and expectations survey	First, second grades: end of year
Anecdotal notes	First, second grades: all year
Field notes, parent meetings	Second grade: monthly

FIG. B-2.   *Data Collected*

Interpreting the data

Each summer during and after the study we went into retreat for several days to immerse ourselves in the data. The first summer we read and shared related literature we had been reading and gathering throughout the year, generated issues, and speculated on connections to our own work. We wrote individual researcher biographies, to "make explicit the point of view [we] brought to the school site and its evolution while [we were] there" (Erickson 1973, p. 60).

We began the interpretation process by reading together the section from *Theoretical Sensitivity* (Glazer 1978) on the questions to keep in mind during coding. We asked each other, "What are these data a study of? What's this story mainly about?" We decided that it was a study of communication among parents, children, and teachers, about expectations, concerns, and the child as a learner. The study had documented ways to support and extend the authenticity of classroom literacy learning, for teachers to learn what was real at home and families to learn what was real at school, and for children to extend their choices in both settings.

First, we read through all the original journals individually, getting a holistic sense of the interactions each represented. Next, we each read the data notebooks we had assembled on each child, which contained a photocopy and a typed transcription of the home-school journals as well as all other information sources. We talked generally about what we noticed, and made general comments about such things as how the specialness of each child came through in every "tell me about your child" letter, how the literacy journals were different across children in response pattern and content yet seemed to be uniformly important to families, and how Betty responded regarding literacy development. We were especially struck by how every family became involved.

Next, we asked Glazer's (1978) coding question "What does this incident indicate?" We coded three home literacy journals together, talking through what we thought was happening entry by entry (Glazer, "What is actually happening here?") There were multiple codes for some incidents; it took about four hours per journal set (a year's dialogue) to do this together. We then generated a sheet of "emerging codes" and subcodes (see Figure B-3), from the very broad to the very specific. Main categories included informing (parent informing teacher, teacher informing parent); supportive statements; response categories, types, and attributes; teacher models, questions, and requests; child response (direct and indirect); and the establishment (or not) of dialogue (usually question/response sequences). Overall, we asked, "What role has this family created for the books and the journal?" Using the emerging codes, we coded a fourth journal set together; we added seven subcodes and clarified two others.

Our retreat over, we agreed to meet once a week, having each coded the same child's journal independently, to compare and reach consensus. Then we reached a very important decision independently but unanimously: We decided we didn't like our analysis process. Betty, the principal investigator, showed up at the first weekly meeting having crystallized the misgivings we were all feeling. She said, "I'm worried that we're missing the forest for the trees. We're breaking these rich interactions down into little codes that become almost meaningless." The agenda for our meeting included the following quotes from Nancie Atwell's *Side by Side* (1991):

Code	Subcode	Meaning
TQ		teacher question
	/Y/N	yes/no
	/auth	author focus
	/lrn	learning focus
	/lks	likes of reader
	/gnr	genre focus (silly books)
	/prc	process (Is C reading book?)
	/eval	evaluation of reading process, development
PC		personal connection
	/RL	real life
	/spec	speculation
	/clss	class discussion reference
Tmod		teacher model (indirect, "fun game," response format)
adTmod		adopted teacher model
exTmod		extended teacher model
NR		no response
NTR		no teacher response
RP		reading process
	/WR	word recognition
	/sp	spelling
	/comp	comprehension
	/eval	evaluation of child's progress, competence
	/WA	word analysis (phonics)
	/phys	physical process (pointing to words)
	/lis	listening
WW		writing workshop, reference to child as writer
Prsp		parent responding
	/bk	book focus ("I like the book")
	/RP	reading process (has subcodes of /WR, /sp, /comp, /eval)
Crsp		child responding (child writing)
	/PW	child responding/parent writing
	Response categories	
	/like	I like the book (often followed by specific category)
	/feel	I feel about the book
	/chr	character
	/evt	events
	/qt	quote
	/pic	picture
	/Wresp	writing of response (handwriting)
	/gnr	genre
	/att	attribute (funny, sad)
	/val	literary values (basal versus real)
	/intp	interpretation ("about good people and bad people")
	Response types	
	/sum	summary
	/ret	retelling
	/pret	partial retelling
	/gist	
	/blrb	like book jacket blurb
	Response attributes	
	/BL	book language
	/inf	inference
	/ref	reflection on response ("How Brandon saw . . . interested")
	/rev	revealed something about the child (doesn't like to be laughed at; indirect)

Code	Subcode	Meaning
Mom		
Dad		
Sib		sibling
Oth		other (family member, neighbor, friend: specify)
TY		thank you (specific kind of SS)
SS		supportive statement ("You're doing a good job, great")
	/T	by teacher to parent
	/P	by parent to teacher
	/T>C	by teacher to child
	/Time	spending time with child
	/Time/R	time reading
	/spec	specific action (writing about feeling)
	/Catt	child attribute (hard worker, good reader)
	/ill	child or parent as illustrator
	/feel	shared feelings about book
	/eff	efficacy
	/emp	empathy
eval		evaluation (− if negative)
TsugB		teacher suggestion of another book to read
ttl		title of book (if title only entry)
auth		author focus in response or SS
TiP		teacher informing parent about child
PiT		parent informing teacher about child
	/exp	possible explanations
	/ins	insight
PtchC		parent teaching child
pers		personal note, not related to journal/literature
pers/sc		personal note, school business, class event
m2m		mother to mother (parent to parent)
inv		invitation to dialogue ("Does this make sense?")
prd		pride in self or other
Dreq		direct request (would you . . . ; has subcodes of /T>P, /T>C, /P>T)
	/Pinv	parent involvement in journal process
	/expl	explicit actions asked for (find tutor, write response)
	/clss	class (asking child to share with class)
	/conv	conventions (punctuation)
	/info	for information
Ireq		indirect request ("I miss your W")
resDreq		response to direct request
resIreq		response to indirect request
	/did	did what other requested
	/did(p)	did part of request
	/ig	ignored request
	/alt	suggested alternative
Chc		choice
	/B	book choice
	/R	who read the book ("He read it to me at his own choice")
PI		peer interaction

Other codes for different kinds of books, e.g., predictable, teacher read aloud, unit-related, may be developed.

FIG. B-3. *Extended Literacy Communities, Emerging Codes, August 1992*

I worry about attempts to package teacher research as another formula to be followed, shutting down the possibility of surprise through a slavish adherence to the conventions of experimental inquiry. . . . Its [classroom research] power lies in thinking side by side with others—our students among them—who care as much about writing, literature, and learning as we do. (p. xvi)

We started thinking about what *is* unique about teacher research. Betty said, "What have we valued most in this team's collaborative review of data—insights or matching boxes?" When JoBeth typed out the code sheet, the analysis became more mechanistic than insightful.

There were at least two flaws in the way we had proceeded: we had not studied the method and its theoretical roots, and we had not verbalized what was important to us as researchers and what that led to methodologically. First, the Glazer and Strauss constant comparative method is intended for something we were not committed to doing: generating grounded theory, which grows out of a deep understanding of and commitment to "symbolic interactionism." We agreed with the social construction of knowledge and world views and with the idea that it is through interaction with others, objects, and self that we "come to know." However, we were more interested in affecting educational practice than in generating theories about it. We wanted to look into an experience that seemed meaningful to all participants and ask, "What made this meaningful? What meanings did different people create from it? What difference for families, children, and teachers did the experience make?"

Second, we had not really stated what it was that we had done that was meaningful, what we wanted to do, and where that would take us in terms of methods. Betty's questions were leading us to that discussion. She proposed a plan that we subsequently modified slightly and used the rest of the year:

1. Separately, each researcher read through the original (photocopied) journals to note illustrations, and so on.
2. Each read the notebooks (which included all data sources) thoroughly, making analytic memos as she read (journal transcripts had three-inch right margins, which helped this process).
3. Each wrote a one- to three-page narrative that included patterns of response and pivotal points of change, questions for further exploration, telling excerpts, and so on (see Figures B-4 to B-6 at the end of this appendix).
4. At dinner meetings (we identified food as essential to our collaboration), we read the narratives aloud to each other, comparing insights, generating new questions, proposing issues and categories.
5. We made a three-column (one for each of us) chart of key insights, points of agreement and difference, and questions. These narratives and charts became the basis of *Engaging Families*.
6. We continued to study the practices of other researchers like Nancie Atwell, Vivan Paley, and Andrew Gitlin.

The process we developed is, we believe, closely related to what Erickson (1986) described as an interpretive research method of data analysis. It is also closely akin to the process Jane Hansen, Donald Graves, and others used in well-known literacy studies (Hubbard and Stratton 1985). In his chapter on qualitative methods in research on teaching, Erickson wrote:

As Hymes notes (1982), interpretive research methods are intrinsically democratic; one does not need special training to be able to understand the results of such research, nor does one need arcane skills in order to conduct it. Fieldwork research requires skills of observation, comparison, contrast, and reflection that all humans possess. In order to get through life we must all do interpretive fieldwork. What professional interpretive researchers do is to make use of ordinary skills of observation and reflection in especially systematic and deliberate ways. Classroom teachers' . . . role is not that of the participant observer who comes from the outside world to visit, but that of an unusually observant participant who deliberates inside the scene of action. (p. 157)

We felt much more true to ourselves, and to our data, with our narrative approach. The dread we had been feeling about the tedium of line-by-line coding was replaced with an eagerness to read, write, ponder, discuss, and interpret. Children, teachers, and family members stayed vital and engaging rather than becoming dissected and codified.

At regular points in our data analysis we stepped back from the individual children and families and asked ourselves, "What are we learning?" Chapter 1 details these emergent assumptions (about ourselves as teachers, about parents, and about children). We continually modified assumptions by rereading the data, exploring discrepant cases, and examining new data. Those assumptions that were consistently supported by the data are represented in the Family Portraits and Literacy Connections parts of the book.

The second summer we rented a house at Lake Hartwell for a week and drafted most of the book. We reread and analyzed the individual narratives and three-column sheets from our weekly meetings, now looking for patterns across families. These patterns form the basis for the Literacy Connections part. Our muses were novels and novel research including *Growing Up Literate* (Taylor and Dorsey-Gaines 1988), *Praying for Sheetrock* (Green 1991), *Turtle Moon* (Hoffman 1992), *Pigs in Heaven* (Kingsolver 1993), and *The Avenue, Clayton City* (Lincoln 1988). We found this mix of books informative and inspirational, the line between well-researched narratives and well-narrated research (especially *Praying for Sheetrock*) a wonderful model.

The third summer teacher-researcher Barbara Everson graciously gave us the use of her condominium at Hilton Head for four days, and we settled into our tried-and-true routine: walk on the beach for an hour, write for three hours, have lunch at the fantastic, down-home Captain's Deli & Seafood Market, swim, write until dinner, eat great seafood (brain food, you know), then read what we had written individually that day for group feedback. The days ended with a moonlit walk on the beach and reading a chapter or two from our books. We were this year inspired by a similar rich mix of readings: Ruthie Bolton's (1994) autobiography *Gal;* Ernest Gaines' (1993) gripping novel of a cynical teacher and an innocent man on death row, *A Lesson Before Dying;* a historical novel, *Women of the Silk* by Gail Tsukiyama (1991); Kim Chernin's (1983) memoir *In My Mother's House;* and Vivian Paley's (1990) *The Boy Who Would Be a Helicopter* (we have been deeply influenced by all the works of this excellent teacher-researcher).

We did "member checks" several times in a variety of ways. At parent meetings we often asked adult family members for their insights, and we tried out some of our interpretations for feedback. We occasionally called parents when we were analyzing data to clarify or interpret events. We talked with children regularly about how they viewed journals and family stories. We sent a copy of each Family Portrait (Adrian, Lakendra, and Cathy) to the families for substantive feedback, and were delighted at the serious and helpful responses. The families were for the most part very pleased with how they were represented. (We honored one parent's edits of her own writing.)

Analysis for us is very closely tied to revision. As we go to press, we still find ourselves analyzing, rethinking, revising, asking new questions, questioning old answers. . . .

I had coffee with Lakendra's mom [Janice] almost every morning. We talked just about her and the things we observed her doing as a reader and learner. We helped each other notice things. It all mattered.

> (10/24) In the story Old McDonald it was just like you said before, she chose this story and her reading is beautiful.

> (11/6) . . . and as always I was pleased. Lakendra is so excited about learning to read and I just love it.

> (12/-) I notice that she miss quite a few in her addition is there a problem with the adding and subtraction?

Lakendra jumped right in there too, writing up to a page of response even in the early months.

This was my favorite journal because everybody—teacher, parent, child—listened to each other (Lakendra even including what Janice said and Ms. Shockley).

> (1/8) I wonder how it would be if when she brings home a book that is a little too hard, you read it first and then let her try it. Let me know how that way works compared to her reading first [in response to *Chicka Chicka Boom Boom*].

> (1/9) Now that's a good idea. I never thought of that but I will try it.

When Lakendra proves to be a proficient responder herself, she still "worries her mother to death about writing in her journal after she reads the story." Could this be like still wanting to be read to even when you can read yourself? Or does Lakendra really need the shot in the arm, so to speak, of support that she gets when her mom actually writes down how proud she is of her.

It is an unreal feeling to have a first grader recommend books by saying "you are to take this book home too" or to show such attachment by composing an entry that oozes issues of engagement, community, and stability.

> (4/30) The book that I took home I alway love this book you are to take this book home some tim this book is very good. Tho do not hit [hide] this from me ok I love this book I am so glid you have good book Ms. Shockley.

Notes:
The thing she likes to do best at home is *homework* [reading, talking, writing in journal].
Likes to fish with her father and her favorite magazine is *Fishing*.
Her biggest worry is her daddy fishing.
[Informal reading inventory] Graph shows strong and steady progress.
Amazing how much she could write about a dog and a cat in 15 minutes.
Mother refers often to our "methods" of teaching. Does she know a difference?
Lakendra says, "When Ms. Shockley learn us how to read she read a lot of book and I love them very very much."

FIG. B-4.   *Betty's Lakendra Narrative*

I thought it was interesting that Lakendra completed the interest inventory you sent for homework at the beginning of school, yet it was November before she attempted to write her own response in the journal. She wrote seven responses in November and December, then didn't write her own response again until the end of March. Over the year Lakendra wrote only twelve responses in her journal; the remainder were written by her mom [Janice].

It is clear that both Lakendra and her mom took their homework seriously. The consistent help and support Lakendra got at home (from mom, dad, and grandfather) surely influenced the progress Lakendra made in her reading. She started the year essentially as a nonreader; by the end of the year she was reading competently.

Mom used the journal to inform Betty of Lakendra's daily progress in reading. She shared concerns she had about how Lakendra was progressing and appreciated Betty's responses to her concerns. This journal is full of examples of Betty's teaching mom about the process of becoming a reader. [Mom] also used the journal to let Betty know how much she appreciated her. This journal is full of praise for everyone involved—Lakendra, Mom, and Betty.

The majority of Mom's responses seem to be based on Lakendra's ability to decode the words in the books she chose. Even when Betty asks her to include Lakendra's ideas and feelings about the books, she continues to report only on Lakendra's decoding ability. Mom stuck to a similar pattern throughout the year.

It is clear that she enjoyed doing this homework with Lakendra. I feel like this daily shared reading was new in their lives. Lakendra reports at the start of the year that she has ten books of her own. I wonder if that has changed after her first-grade experience with so much reading at home. I also wonder if Lakendra and her mom discussed the stories they read. There didn't seem to be any personal connections made with the books Lakendra brought home.

This year Lakendra has had difficulty comprehending what she reads. I noticed this and became more aware of it through the countywide assessment we are using. Her mom also noticed this difficulty and is working on having more discussion about the books they read at home. Lakendra is still reluctant to write her own responses in her journal. Mom continues to write about their reading time together.

FIG. B-5.   *Barbara's Lakendra Narrative*

This journal is about relationships. It highlights a mother-daughter relationship of love, support, and challenge; it is also the vehicle for a relationship between Janice and Betty. Both are openly appreciative of the other. Janice thanks Betty in general with almost every entry, and several times thanks her specifically. She wrote, "I'm glad to know Fowler Drives Teacher is so good and patient with there students especially you. I'm glad to know I don't have to worry about Lakendra in your class" (11/7) and thanks her again for "your good work of teaching" (2/19). She shares some of herself, although infrequently. On March 11, after Betty had reported Lakendra's narration (in front of the whole class) of a play, Janice wrote, "I please to know Lakendra is very out spoken me myself when I had to do a play or something in school I was very shy. . . ." In turn, Betty frequently offers supportive statements of Janice's efficacy both as a parent ("a wonderful mother!") and a teacher (time, support, her own enjoyment of reading, and specific strategies, such as knowing when to take over the reading herself when Lakendra is struggling).

Janice sees herself as a teacher too. Several of the exchanges really seem teacher to teacher. She confers with Betty several times about reading processes, like her worry that Lakendra is singing rather than reading the words. Betty offers concrete recommendations, support for risk taking, and constant support of Janice as her daughter's home teacher. Janice has a special concern with the difficulty of the books. She seems to have a strong sense of instructional level—she doesn't want books that are either too easy or too difficult. Betty counters that kids still learn from easy books and that Janice can take over the reading when the books are too difficult. Janice follows up on suggestions to read to her daughter when the books are difficult or when Lakendra asks her to. Still, Janice seems to prefer books that are slightly challenging but that Lakendra can read with a little help—working right in that old ZPD!

Early on, Janice seems to defer to Betty's expertise, but during the math exchanges she politely holds her opinion. She understands what Betty is saying about maturation, " . . . but could you please send Lakendra some problems or work sheet so she can practice it too. I would appreciate it." In the next entry, after no response, she wrote, "I understand what you are saying I'm just concerned about her adding and subtracting."

In her last entry, Janice wrote, "I really think that student journal is a great way for the parents and teachers to communicate with each other. . . . I really enjoyed it." She has her finger on the primary use of the journal, which seemed to be to *inform*. The principal codes were *parent informing teacher* and *teacher informing parent*. They provided both general evaluation (almost always about reading progress, how well Lakendra was doing) and specific insights, such as pointing to the words, singing or memorizing versus reading, and so on. Information was often about the reading process, although both mentioned the writing process as well.

Betty and Janice share a vision of what reading should be: enjoyable. Both use the term frequently. This was Betty's primary goal, that parents and children enjoy their time together around books; Janice and Lakendra obviously do. Once Lakendra even wrote, "I love this book Ms. Shockley do you love [this book—appears to be added by mom] It make me so so happy I hope you injony it" (4/1).

There were several shifts in the journal. It began with a very consistent format of Janice telling Betty that Lakendra was progressing well as a reader and then adding information or questions related to her reading process. The responses did not focus on the content of the books, but on the reading event. Betty responded in kind. On

(continued)

October 23, Betty made a direct request for a change in response, writing, "Remember to include Lakendra's ideas and feelings in these responses." There was no direct change, but on November 5, Lakendra wrote for the first time. She continued to write her own responses periodically throughout the year, although Janice was obviously very involved, often prefacing Lakendra's remarks with her own. Betty encourages them both to write in the journal, which they do. Both adults use the journal to share occasional concerns and information not directly related to the night's reading, as when Betty remarks on classroom events and when Janice asks about math and the Christmas party.

Betty tried again in February to get content-oriented responses. There has been only one, on January 9, when Janice wrote, "The story left both of us asking the question of who's big toe was it." When Betty prompted for what Lakendra says about the books, Janice responded, "I still can't get her to tell me in sequence that good but we are working on it" (2/12). Has she interpreted Betty's prompts to mean a traditional comprehension Q/A? Betty tried one more time, in April, by modeling a book-specific response: "I think it served the lion right to fall in the river. He shouldn't be bossing the other animals around like that even if he is king of the jungle!" There is no noticeable effect.

There is growth in Lakendra's responding, both in types of responses and in the conventions of writing. Her most pervasive response type is general evaluation: "It was good." [Betty—there seems to be a lot on 11/5—can you help decode it? Is she talking about finding new good book with a good family, and/or writing her own book?] She often includes dialogue of the "do you like it/yes I do" variety, and sometimes "seard lakendra." One interesting and diverse response is on November 14, when she reports that she liked the story but "my mom do not"; that shows us that they were really discussing the story and that Lakendra knows that people can have different opinions about books. In December, Lakendra includes the author (Marc Brown). She demonstrates a reading community membership in several ways; she includes "reviews" by others ("This book is terrific that Renee took home I bet she like it too" 4/28), asks Betty to take books home to read, and reads a book by a peer. Her spelling, punctuation, and sentence sense improve greatly by the end of the year.

Lakendra has a genuine audience of appreciative adults, primarily her mother but also her father and grandfather. They marvel over her ability—this child who is in Chapter 1 reading at school is seen as an accomplished reader at home. At the end of the year, Mom announces, "I think she's got reading down pack!" In a comment that Betty has already immortalized, Lakendra wrote, "I love thm whnen they lisn to me." I don't know if this is a family that reads a lot, but it is definitely a family that values its daughter's literacy. Janice takes real risks in her own writing; she writes twice in an apologetic way about her spelling and penmanship. She trusts that Betty is really interested in what she has to say, not how she says it.

I loved it when Janice wrote on January 7, "Lakendra read the story Bells or maybe a reading book"—Mom knows the difference.

FIG. B-6. *JoBeth's Lakendra Narrative*

REFERENCES

Allen, J., B. Michalove, and B. Shockley. 1993. *Engaging children: Community and chaos in the lives of young literacy learners*. Portsmouth, N.H.: Heinemann.

Atwell, N. 1991. *Side by side: Essays on teaching to learn*. Portsmouth, N.H.: Heinemann.

Baker, L., J. Allen, B. Shockley, T. Pellegrini, L. Galda, and S. Stahl. In press. Connecting school and home: Constructing partnerships to foster reading development. In *Developing engaged readers in school and home communities*, ed. L. Baker, P. Afflerbach, and D. Reinking. Hillsdale, N.J.: Erlbaum.

Belenky, M., B. Clinchy, N. Goldberger, and J. Tarule. 1986. *Women's ways of knowing: The development of self, voice, and mind*. New York: Basic Books.

Bronfenbrenner, U. 1979. *The ecology of human development*. Cambridge, Mass.: Harvard University Press.

Calkins, L. 1986. *The art of teaching writing*. Portsmouth, N.H.: Heinemann.

———. 1991. *Living between the lines*. Portsmouth, N.H.: Heinemann.

Cambourne, B. 1988. *The whole story: Natural learning and the acquisition of literacy in the classroom*. New York: Scholastic.

Carr, E., and J. Allen. 1989. University/classroom teacher collaboration: Costs, benefits, and mutual respect. In *Qualitative research in education*, ed. J. Goetz and J. Allen. Athens, Ga.: University of Georgia, College of Education.

Cullinan, B., and L. Galda. 1994. *Literature and the child*. Fort Worth: Harcourt, Brace.

Delpit, L. 1991. A conversation with Lisa Delpit. *Language Arts 68:* 541–547.

Dillon, D. 1989. Dear readers. *Language Arts* 66(1): 7–9.

Durkin, D. 1966. *Children who read early*. New York: Teachers College Press.

Eeds, M., and M. Peterson. 1990. *Grand conversations: Literature groups in action*. New York: Scholastic.

Erickson, F. 1973. What makes school ethnography "ethnographic"? *Council of Anthropology and Education Quarterly,* 4(2): 10–19.

———. 1986. Qualitative methods in research on teaching. In *Handbook of research on teaching,* 3d ed., ed. M. C. Wittrock. New York: Macmillan.

Fitzgerald, L. M., and A. Goncu. In press. Parent involvement in urban early childhood education: A Vygotskian approach. In *Advances in early education and day care: A research annual,* ed. S. Reitel. Greenwich, Conn.: JAI Press.

Fletcher, R. 1993. *What a writer needs*. Portsmouth, N.H.: Heinemann.

Fox, M. 1992. Once upon a time there were three . . . *The New Advocate* 5: 165–174.

Fraatz, J.M.B. 1987. *The politics of reading: Power, opportunity, and prospects for change in America's public schools*. New York: Teachers College Press.

Glazer, B. 1978. *Theoretical sensitivity*. Mill Valley, Calif.: Sociology Press.

Goldenberg, C. 1989. Making success a more common occurrence for children at risk for failure: Lessons from Hispanic first graders learning to read. In *Risk makers, risk takers, risk breakers: Reducing the risks for young literacy learners,* ed. J. Allen and J. Mason. Portsmouth, N.H.: Heinemann.

Graves, D. 1990. *Discover your own literacy.* Portsmouth, N.H.: Heinemann.

Hansen, J. 1989. Anna evaluates herself. In *Risk makers, risk takers, risk breakers: Reducing the risks for young literacy learners,* ed. J. Allen and J. Mason. Portsmouth, N.H.: Heinemann.

Heath, S. B. 1983. *Ways with words.* Cambridge: Cambridge University Press.

Heilbrun, C. G. 1988. *Writing a woman's life.* New York: Norton.

Hubbard, R., and D. Stratton, eds. 1985. *Teachers and learners and other narratives of the Mast Way Research Project.* Durham, N.H.: Writing Process Lab.

Huck, C., S. Hepler, and J. Hickman. 1993. *Children's literature in the elementary school.* 5th ed. Orlando, Fla.: Holt, Rinehart and Winston.

Hymes, D. 1982. Ethnographic monitoring. In *Culture in the bilingual classroom,* ed. H. T. Treuba, G. P. Guthrie, and K. H. Au. Rowley, Mass.: Newbury House.

McLaughlin, M., and P. Shields. 1987. Involving low-income parents in the schools: A role for policy? *Phi Delta Kappan* (October): 156–160.

Moll, L., C. Amanti, D. Neff, and N. Gonzalez. 1992. Funds of knowledge for teaching: Using a qualitative approach to connect homes and classrooms. *Theory into Practice* 31(2): 132–141.

Oldfather, P. 1993. What students say about motivating experiences in a whole language classroom. *The Reading Teacher* 46(8): 672–681.

Paley, V. 1990. *The boy who would be a helicopter.* Cambridge, Mass.: Harvard University Press.

Peterson, R. 1992. *Life in a crowded place: Making a learning community.* Portsmouth, N.H.: Heinemann.

Sarason, S. 1982. *The culture of the school and the problem of change.* Boston, Mass.: Allyn and Bacon.

Sattes, B. 1985. *Parent involvement: A review of the literature.* Occasional Paper No. 21. Charleston, W.V.: Appalachia Educational Laboratory.

Shockley, B. 1993. Extending the literate community: Reading and writing with families. *The New Advocate* 6(1): 11–23.

Short, K., and K. Pierce. 1990. *Talking about books: Creating literate communities.* Portsmouth, N.H.: Heinemann.

Skolnick, D. F. 1992. Reading relationships. *The New Advocate* 5(2): 117–127.

Smith, F. 1988. *Joining the literacy club.* Portsmouth, N.H.: Heinemann.

Swap, S. 1993. *Developing home-school partnerships.* New York: Teachers College Press.

Taylor, D., and C. Dorsey-Gaines. 1988. *Growing up literate: Learning from inner-city families.* Portsmouth, N.H.: Heinemann.

Taylor, D., and D. S. Strickland. 1986. *Family storybook reading.* Portsmouth, N.H.: Heinemann.

———. 1989. Learning from families: Implications for educators and policy. In *Risk makers, risk takers, risk breakers: Reducing the risks for young literacy learners,* ed. J. Allen and J. Mason. Portsmouth, N.H.: Heinemann.

Vygotsky, L. 1978. *Mind in society.* Cambridge, Mass.: Harvard University Press.

Yaden, D., L. Smolkin, A. Conlan. 1989. Preschoolers' questions about pictures, print convention, and story text during reading aloud at home. *Reading Research Quarterly* 24(2): 188–214.

LITERATURE CITED

Adler, D. A. Various dates. Cam Jansen mysteries. New York: Viking.

Andersen, H. C. 1949. *The emperor's new clothes*. Boston: Houghton Mifflin.

Bare, C. S. 1989. *Critter, the class cat*. New York: Putnam.

Bolton, R. M. 1994. *Gal: A true life*. New York: Harcourt, Brace.

Bond, F. 1983. *The Halloween performance*. New York: Scholastic.

Boo Bear and the kite. 1986. In *Drums*. Boston: Houghton Mifflin.

The boy who fooled the giant. 1994. Los Angeles: Wonder.

Breathed, B. 1991. *A wish for wings that work*. Boston: Little, Brown.

Bridwell, N. 1963. *Clifford, the big red dog*. New York: Four Winds.

Brown, K. 1990. *Why can't I fly?* New York: Doubleday.

Brown, M. T. 1979. *Arthur's eyes*. Boston: Little, Brown.

———. 1983. *Spooky riddles*. New York: Beginner.

Brown, M. W. 1993. *Goodnight moon*. New York: Scholastic.

Buchanan, D. A. 1991. *Mr. Grumpuss*. New York: Vantage.

Bulla, C. R. 1966. *White bird*. New York: Crowell.

Burns, D. L., and C. Burns. 1989. *Hail to the chief! Jokes about the presidents*. Minneapolis: Lerner.

Calmenson, S. 1989. *The principal's new clothes*. New York: Scholastic.

Cameron, A. 1981. *The stories Julian tells*. New York: Pantheon.

Carle, E. 1976. *The very hungry caterpillar*. Cleveland: Collins and World.

Chernin, K. 1983. *In my mother's house*. New York: Harper and Row.

Cole, B. 1986. *The giant's toe*. Toronto: Collins.

Cowley, J. 1986. *The spaceship*. San Diego: Wright Group.

Dalgliesh, A. 1952. *The bears on Hemlock Mountain*. New York: Scribner.

Dahl, R. 1970. *Fantastic Mr. Fox*. New York: Knopf.

———. 1982. *The BFG*. New York: Farrar, Straus, Giroux.

Delton, J. 1993. *PeeWee scouts: Piles of pets*. South Holland, Ill.: Dell.

Demarest, C. L. 1991. *Kitman and Willy at sea*. New York: Simon and Schuster.

DePaola, T. 1975. *Strega Nona*. Englewood Cliffs, N.J.: Prentice Hall.

———. 1978. *The clown of God: An old story*. New York: Harcourt Brace Jovanovich.

Dewey, A. 1983. *Pecos Bill*. New York: Greenwillow.

Dodds, S. 1988. *Charles Tiger*. Boston: Little, Brown.

Domico, T. 1988. *Bears of the world*. New York: Facts on File.

Dorros, A. 1982. *Alligator shoes*. New York: Dutton.

Doyle, A. C. 1892. *Adventures of Sherlock Holmes*. New York: Grosset and Dunlap.

Eastman, P. D. 1960. *Are you my mother?* New York: Random.

Ehle, J. 1989. *The widow's trial*. New York: Harper.

Family stories. 1992. Written by Betty Shockley's first-grade families, Fowler Drive Elementary School, Athens, Ga. Available from authors.

Fremont, E. 1992. *Jokes from the crypt*. New York: Random House.

Gaines, E. 1993. *A lesson before dying*. New York: Vintage.

Giff, P. 1989. *Garbage juice for breakfast*. New York: Dell.

Godden, R. 1970. *The old woman who lived in a vinegar bottle*. New York: Viking.

Green, M. F. 1991. *Praying for sheetrock: A work of nonfiction*. Reading, Mass.: Addison-Wesley.

Grisham, J. 1991. *The firm*. New York: Doubleday.

Hayward, L. 1990. *All stuck up*. New York: Random.

Hirst, R., and S. Hirst. 1988. *My place in space*. Illus. by R. Harvey with J. Levine. New York: Orchard.

Hoffman, A. 1992. *Turtle moon*. New York: Putnam.

Hort, L. 1991. *How many stars in the sky?* New York: Morrow.

Hutchins, P. 1967. *Rosie's walk*. New York: Macmillan.

———. 1986. *The doorbell rang*. New York: Greenwillow.

Jeschke, S. 1980. *Perfect the pig*. New York: Holt.

Johnson, S. 1991. *Hermit crabs*. Minneapolis: Lerner.

Katz, B. 1989. *Poems for small friends*. New York: Random.

Kay, T. 1981. *After Eli*. Boston: Houghton Mifflin.

Kellogg, S. 1985. *Chicken little*. New York: Morrow.

King-Smith, D. 1988. *Martin's mice*. New York: Crown.

Kingsolver, B. 1993. *Pigs in heaven: A novel*. New York: HarperCollins.

Krauss, R. 1992. *I can fly*. Racine, Wis.: Western Publishing.

Lincoln, C. E. 1988. *The avenue, Clayton City*. New York: Morrow.

Lionni, L. 1968. *The biggest house in the world*. New York: Pantheon.

———. 1989. *Tillie and the wall*. New York: Knopf.

Littledale, F. 1980. *The magic fish*. Sydney, Australia: Ashton Scholastic.

Lobel, A. 1979. *Days with frog and toad*. New York: Harper.

Mann, A. W. 1950. *The Jackie Robinson story*. New York: F. J. Low Co.

Marshall, J. 1976. *George and Martha rise and shine*. Boston: Houghton Mifflin.

———. 1982. *Fox and his friends*. New York: Dial.

———. 1983. *Rapscallion Jones*. New York: Viking.

———. 1988. *Goldilocks and the three bears*. New York: Dial.

———. 1994. *Fox in love*. New York: Puffin.

Martin, B. 1989. *Chicka chicka boom boom*. New York: Simon and Schuster.

Mathis, S. B. 1975. *The hundred penny box*. New York: Viking.

Mills, C. 1983. *The secret carousel*. New York: Four Winds.

Mozelle, S. 1989. *Zack's alligator*. New York: HarperCollins.

Parrish, P. 1985. *Amelia Bedelia goes camping*. New York: Greenwillow.

Potter, B. 1963. *The tale of Peter Rabbit*. Racine, Wis.: Golden.

The punisher. New York: Marvel Entertainment Group.

Raffi. 1987. *Down by the bay*. New York: Crown.

Rey, H. A. 1957. *Curious George gets a medal*. Boston: Houghton Mifflin.

Reynolds, P. 1993. *The book of silly lists*. New York: Watermill.

Rounds, G. 1989. *Old MacDonald had a farm*. New York: Holiday.

San Souci, R. 1989. *The talking eggs: A folktale from the American South*. New York: Dial.

Schanback, M. 1990. *Does third grade last forever?* Mahwah, N.J.: Troll.

Schulman, J. 1978. *Jack the bum and the UFO*. New York: Greenwillow.

Science. First-grade textbook. Reading, Mass.: Addison-Wesley.

Scieszka, J. 1991. *The frog prince continued*. New York: Viking.

———. 1991. *Knights of the kitchen table*. Time Warp Trio Series. New York: Viking.

———. 1991. *The-not-so-jolly Roger*. Time Warp Trio Series. New York: Viking.

Scieszka, J. 1992. *The true story of the three little pigs*. New York: Viking.

Sendak, M. 1962. *Chicken soup with rice*. New York: HarperCollins.

Shepard, E. 1952. *Paul Bunyan*. New York: Harcourt, Brace and World.

Smiley, J. 1991. *A thousand acres*. New York: Knopf.

Spier, P. 1961. *Fox went out on a chilly night: An old song*. Garden City, N.Y.: Doubleday.

Stories from our lives. 1992. Written by Barbara Michalove's second-grade families, Fowler Drive Elementary School, Athens, Ga. Available from authors.

Strickland, C. 1993. *Star the horse*. Available from authors.

Thomson, P. 1988. *Can you hear me, Grandad?* New York: Delacorte.

Tsukiyama, G. 1991. *Women of the silk*. New York: St. Martin's.

Van Laan, N. 1990. *Possum come a-knockin'*. New York: Knopf.

Ward, C. 1988. *Cookie's week*. New York: Putnam.

Warner, G. C. 1950. *Boxcar children*. Boxcar Children Mysteries. Morton Grove, Ill.: A. Whitman.

———. (19561). *Blue Bay mystery*. Boxcar Children Mysteries. Morton Grove, Ill.: A. Whitman.

Wells, R. 1986. *Max's Christmas*. New York: Dial.

White, E. B. 1952. *Charlotte's web*. New York: Harper.

Wilder, L. I. 1932. *Little house in the big woods*. New York: Harper.

Wilder, L. I. 1935. *Little house on the prairie*. New York: Harper.

Williams, K. L. 1990. *Galimoto*. New York: Lothrop, Lee and Shepard.

Winter, J. 1988. *Follow the drinking gourd*. New York: Knopf.

Wood, D. 1991. *Piggies*. San Diego: Harcourt Brace Jovanovich.

Wood, D., and A. Wood. 1987. *Heckedy peg*. San Diego: Harcourt Brace Jovanovich.

Wyler, R., and G. Ames. 1991. *Magic secrets*. New York: HarperCollins.

Yolen, J. 1978. *No bath tonight*. New York: Crowell.